Music: A Very Short Introduction

VERY SHORT INTRODUCTIONS are for anyone wanting a stimulating and accessible way into a new subject. They are written by experts, and have been translated into more than 45 different languages.

The series began in 1995, and now covers a wide variety of topics in every discipline. The VSI library currently contains over 650 volumes—a Very Short Introduction to everything from Psychology and Philosophy of Science to American History and Relativity—and continues to grow in every subject area.

Very Short Introductions available now:

Nicholas Cook

MUSIC

A Very Short Introduction

SECOND EDITION

OXFORD
UNIVERSITY PRESS

Great Clarendon Street, Oxford, OX2 6DP,
United Kingdom

Oxford University Press is a department of the University of Oxford.
It furthers the University's objective of excellence in research, scholarship,
and education by publishing worldwide. Oxford is a registered trade mark of
Oxford University Press in the UK and in certain other countries

First published 1998
Reissued 2000
This edition published 2021

Impression: 1

Published in the United States of America by Oxford University Press
198 Madison Avenue, New York, NY 10016, United States of America

British Library Cataloguing in Publication Data
Data available

Library of Congress Control Number: 2020945706

ISBN 978-0-19-872604-3

Printed in Great Britain by
Ashford Colour Press Ltd, Gosport, Hampshire

Contents

Acknowledgements

My thanks go to Tom McAuley, Ariana Phillips-Hutton, and an anonymous referee for their helpful comments on a draft version of this book; to the graduate students, postdoctoral researchers, and colleagues at the University of Cambridge and elsewhere who introduced me to new topics and ideas; and to the many readers of the original edition who got in touch with me, whether to correct mistakes, make suggestions, or ask for help with their homework. I also thank Jenny Nugee and Bhavani Govindasamy for their help and tolerance during the production process.

List of illustrations

Introduction

'I want to be … *a musician*'. Those are the first words of a
forty-second television commercial for Prudential pension plans
that begins with a headphoned young man dreaming of his future.
It proceeds through a series of juxtapositions. First his imagined
words are answered by his father ('You want to be earning your
keep, my son'). Then he tells us he wants to cut his first album
(we see him cutting grass at a local park). He wants to be packing
them in at Wembley (we see him packing breakfast cereals at a
supermarket). Now we see his fantasy: he is playing in a jazz/rock
band, the camera zooming in on him at a grand piano. Behind
him are two glamorous vocalists. But suddenly the scene cuts to
Whiteley's shopping centre in Bayswater. He is still at the piano
but the glamorous vocalists have turned into two middle-aged
women, one of whom asks him 'Do you know "I want to be
Bobby's girl"?' 'Oh no', he mutters.

We don't hear any of this music. Instead we hear a slow, singing
melody in a classical style, four balanced phrases that proceed
naturally but inevitably to a conclusion whose final notes
coincide with the Prudential logo. (The commercial is one of a
long-running series featuring this music.) Just like the gulf
between fantasy and reality, so the opposition between the band

and classical music expresses the contradictory values the commercial is all about: youth and freedom on the one hand, as symbolized by the young man's aspiration to become a musician, and on the other hand the sensible but dull world of his father and pension plans. Standing for personal expression and truth to yourself, the band targets the demographic at which the commercial is aimed. Meanwhile a reassuringly authoritative voice superimposed on the classical melody explains how you may go through a number of jobs, but you can take your Prudential pension plan with you. Together the voiceover and the melody's drive towards its conclusion create the commercial's message: you need to think about how you are going to provide for your old age—but don't worry, Prudential have the solution. The music proves it.

This commercial goes back to the 1990s, and I used it to kick off the original version of *Music: A Very Short Introduction*, which first appeared in 1998. Its televisual style looks quite old-fashioned now. But some things don't change and among them is music's ability to convey complex cultural meanings. Music encodes values, our cherished beliefs about the world we live in. It penetrates deep into our emotions, our feelings, our sense of who we are and who we want to be. It targets people: the voiceover gives the facts, but it is music that speaks confidentially, to you alone. It persuades. And it can do all this without your being aware of it. Music is an entertainment, one of life's great pleasures, but it also penetrates deep into culture and identity.

So this new version of the book shares some of its genes with the old one. It has the same emphasis on music as culture, as something we make, think about, and think *in*. It even has some of the same examples. But many things have changed since 1998 and so I have completely rewritten it. Digital technology has changed pretty much everything in the world of music; there is a chapter about this, but it runs through much of the book. Again, the world becomes ever more globalized, and the book reflects that. And there is a lot more emphasis on music as a practice of real-time performance.

I intended this new edition to be how I would have written the original book if I had been writing it today. But today has arrived and it is not what I or anybody else expected. The book is going to press in November 2020, at the height of the Covid-19 pandemic, when across the world restrictions on social gatherings have brought live performance—and with it most musicians' income streams—to a juddering halt. Performing arts companies are pleading for governmental support, issuing dire warnings about the future of live theatre, dance, and music if their calls are not heeded. Choral singing has been identified as a source of super-spreading. In Britain the BBC has put on orchestral performances where the players are all two metres apart and audiences are listening at home; these socially distanced events create a new kind of orchestral sound, with less emphasis on blend and more on the contribution of individual players. And across all genres and traditions, musicians are experimenting as never before with telematic music (music created in real time by physically separated musicians linked via the internet). You might expect the big winner to be streaming services, but even they have suffered through the slashing of advertising budgets. What effect will all this have in the coming years? Will 2020 come to be seen as a turning point in the history of music? Or as just a temporary aberration that in the end didn't change so much? By the time you read this book you may have a better idea of the answers to these questions than I do.

Chapter 1
Music in the moment

Growing older together

Google 'music', and along with about 9,690,000,000 other hits you might find Figures 1 and 2. Which of them is the music? Is it an activity, something people do, or a product, something people make? In the West (a problematic term by which I roughly mean

1. **The Guarneri String Quartet (Arnold Steinhardt is on the left).**

Europe, the Americas, and the larger anglophone world) there is a long tradition of thinking of music less as an activity than as a product. It wasn't until the late 20th century that the music educator Christopher Small redressed the balance by coining the verb 'musicking' to refer unambiguously to the activity. But the sense that music exists on two planes, or as two parallel worlds, is implicit in the French philosopher Jean-Paul Sartre's observation that if the concert hall burns down during a performance of Ludwig van Beethoven's Seventh Symphony, the symphony does not cease to exist. Music as product is not tied to time and space, but music as activity happens in the here and now.

You might call music an art of time, perhaps of all cultural practices the one most intimately tied to time. In the collective

2. Opening of Mozart's String Quartet in G major, K 387, as published by Breitkopf & Härtel (Leipzig) in 1882. This is one of a series of late 19th-century editions of what by then were seen as the masterworks of classical music, aiming to represent them in an authoritative and permanent form.

improvisation of jazz, musicians are (more or less) making up the music as they go along, and they do this by constantly listening to one another. But it's not just jazz. In any tradition or genre, making music together is an art of split-second interaction. Arnold Steinhardt, first violinist of the Guarneri Quartet, speaks of his first experience of playing in a string quartet. He and three fellow students at the Curtis Institutite of Music in Philadelphia were assigned Wolfgang Amadeus Mozart's Quartet K 387 (the K stands for Ludwig von Köchel, who created the authoritative catalogue of Mozart's music, and 387 is the number he gave this quartet). Steinhardt's part looked ridiculously easy—he already had a virtuoso technique—but after a few minutes he had changed his mind:

> The ensemble was chaotic and we all missed cues ... If this was such easy music, why was I stumbling over notes, making a poor sound, and having such trouble with the simple rhythms?

When performed, the music that on paper was a simple succession of notes one after another turned out to be an intricate web of cues, demanding close listening and instant response. In performance, time is dynamic, flexible, and situational: it seems to flow faster or slower depending on the music. And more than that, it is social. Through their interactions performers share musical time with one another, as well as with the audience. In a word, they negotiate it. You keep in time not by adhering to your own beat and expecting everyone else to fall in with you, but by listening to everyone else and adjusting to them as they adjust to you; that's why in both jazz and string quartets the worst thing you can say about someone is they don't listen. It is this web of relationships that produces musical time.

If you think about time you will almost certainly think about music. Writing in 1951 about intersubjectivity, the German sociologist Alfred Schutz contrasted clock time, in which every second is the same and a minute lasts 60 times as long, with the time in which we experience music—the time that is dynamic, negotiated, and socially produced. As Schutz put it, anticipating the hippy language of the following decade, 'performer and listener are "tuned-in" to one another, are living together through the same flux, are growing older together while the musical process lasts'.

There is a striking echo of this when two contemporary British sociologists (Elizabeth Hallam and Tim Ingold) speak of the mutual relationships 'through which, as they grow older together, [people] continually participate in each other's coming-into-being'. We live our lives in this socially shared time, they say—a time that 'grows, issuing forth from its advancing tip rather like a root or creeper probes the earth'. People think of their lives as a kind of map across which they chart their course, a space in which you can look back at the past while the future lies over there. But in reality life is not like this: there is no future just waiting to be revealed, and we live each moment as it comes. We get through life by constantly going forward into an unknown future and responding to whatever happens as best we can, that is, by improvising: 'improvisation and creativity', Hallam and Ingold say, 'are intrinsic to the very processes of social and cultural life'. Life cannot be scripted. We may have plans but in the end we make things up as we go along.

Improvisation is equally a fundamental dimension of music's existence in real time. On the printed page music is a series of notes fixed in the same relationships for all time. But as played and heard, music is (in social psychologist Kenneth Gergen's words) a world of 'endless movement, not discrete "forms" but continuous "forming"', a world of lived experience in which human relationships are played out in their most essential, stripped down form. Jazz improvisation in particular has often been seen as offering the vision of an equal society in which there are no leaders, no followers, no hierarchies, no rules except those of working and playing together in harmony. And critically in the context of America, where jazz originated, it was seen as offering the vision of a colour-blind society.

In 1945 the Black poet, folklorist, and Harvard professor Sterling Brown spoke of the democracy in action of 'jam sessions, both public and private, where Negro and white musicians meet as equals to improvise collectively and create the kind of music they love. Here the performer's color does not matter.' Sometimes this utopian view of jazz improvisation is contrasted with the bureaucratic paperwork, rules, regulations, and hierarchies of the Western classical (or 'art music') tradition, where composers prescribe what performers are to play and conductors are there to enforce compliance. Some people, such as the jazz commentator Ben Sidran, have seen the opposed cultures of jazz and classical music as expressing the fundamentally distinct mentalities of 'oral man' and 'literate man' (and woman, presumably): a culture of joyous social extemporization in contrast to one based on the slavish reproduction of authorized texts. For Sidran, orality is linked to 'the peculiarly "black" approach to rhythm', which gives rise to the suspicion that these binaries—oral versus literary, improvisation versus reproduction, jazz versus classical—might simply boil down to race.

But music disrupts this kind of black-and-white thinking. It often attracts idealized interpretations that have little basis in reality, and among them is the idea that improvisation can be genuinely free in the sense of owing nothing to past tradition. Coinciding with the civil rights movement of the 1950s and 60s, there developed a genre called 'free jazz' ('free improvisation' in Europe). It consciously rejected the basic features of the then dominant bebop style, such as regular song-based forms, metres, recognizable harmonic sequences, and even the conventional sonorities of instruments such as the saxophone. Improvisation was seen as central to its freedom, but in practice free jazz drew on multiple aspects of earlier, pre-bebop styles along with others drawn from traditions outside the West. By reconfiguring these elements in new ways, artists like John Coltrane and Ornette Coleman stepped outside the norms of contemporary bebop style. But they did not free themselves from the past.

The point is underlined by another kind of free improvisation that developed at the same time but on the other side of the Atlantic. This came out of the classical (or 'art' music) tradition, and took the form of improvisation ensembles determined to eradicate every trace of tradition from their playing. The post-war modernist composer Pierre Boulez made fun of the vacuous music this gave rise to: at first there would be some excitement, he said,

> and so everybody just made more activity, more activity, louder, louder, louder. Then they were tired so for two minutes you had calm, calm, calm, calm, calm. And then somebody was waking up so they began again, and then they were tired, sooner this time, and so the rest was longer.

This may not have been entirely fair, but Boulez had a point. If you try to improvise in the sense of just playing without any preconceptions, you fall back into engrained mannerisms. You end up imitating yourself. As Charlie Mingus, the double bassist, pianist, composer, and bandleader, supposedly told the self-styled guru of psychedelia, Tim Leary, 'You can't improvise on nothin', man. You gotta improvise on somethin'.' The ethnomusicologist Bruno Nettl has expressed the same thought in more academic terms: 'It may be stated as an article of faith that improvisers always have a point of departure, something which they use to improvise.'

This explains the traditional jazz practice of basing performances on 'standards', well-known songs from American popular culture. Sometimes the players incorporate part or all of a tune, sometimes just a sequence of chord changes, but in either case the result is a framework of shared expectations that underlies the soloists' improvisations. The soloists interact with other band members and with the audience, but they may also incorporate references to famous improvisations on records, or weave in any of the multitude of familiar 'ideas, licks, tricks, pet patterns, crips, clichés, and, in the most functional language, things you can do' that ethnomusicologist Paul Berliner describes as the building blocks of jazz tradition. And it is not just jazz musicians who do this. Another ethnomusicologist, Laudan Nooshin, speaks of the internalized store of ideas and patterns accumulated over a lifetime that forms the basis of Iranian music, in which improvisation and the performance of pre-existing music are inextricably intertwined. Examples could be multiplied from across the world.

In this way improvisation and the performance of pre-existing music are not as distinct as people think. Consider one of the most famous jazz improvisers, Louis Armstrong (aka Satchmo). In 1920s America you had to submit a score in order to claim copyright on your music, so Armstrong submitted written-out versions of his solos two or three years before he 'improvised' them on recordings. The scores and recordings match almost exactly. And if jazz improvisation turns out not to be simply made up on the spot—if it is a weaving together of pre-existing tunes, harmonic patterns, and other formulae—then conversely the performance of pre-existing works turns out to be closer to improvisation than Sidran's sharp division between 'oral' and 'literate' man would suggest. Steinhardt's and his fellow students' problem at that first rehearsal was they didn't know how to negotiate time with one another. In that sense—and it is a key sense—they didn't know how to improvise.

Nor is it just time that is negotiated in performance. Violins, viola, and cellos—the instruments of the string quartet—have no frets, and players continually adjust their intonation to one another to produce the overall sonority they want. They also adjust their dynamic balance in line with the music's changing textures as well as the surging and ebbing of the musical flow. When you listen to K 387, you are not just hearing Mozart's notes: you are hearing a constantly changing web of human relationships (and that is why people keep on listening even when—as the phrase goes—they know the music backwards). The performers may be playing the notes as printed in the score, but at the same time they are playing by ear.

Actually the idea that classical performers play the notes is itself an oversimplification, and when I say that I am not talking about mistakes. As an example, music in the 18th century was commonly written down in the form of a blueprint (in jazz you would call it a lead sheet), with the tune, a bass line, and sometimes figures to indicate the harmonies. Typically the tune would be played by a violinist or woodwind player, and the bassline by a cellist or gamba player. But there would also be a third performer—probably at a harpsichord but perhaps a small organ or lute—who doubled the bass line and filled out the harmonies, often adding shadowy inner parts. There is an obvious parallel between this instrumental grouping and the saxophone, string bass, and piano of a typical jazz quartet ('quartet' because in jazz there is also a drummer).

And the parallel does not stop there. In the 18th-century trio sonata, as it was called, the third (or continuo) player had considerable freedom in realizing the figured bass. By no means was it a simple matter of playing the notes. And the violinist or woodwind player had still more freedom. Particularly in slow movements it was expected that solo performers would extemporize freely on what was written in the score, at the least adding conventional ornamentation or filling in leaps with scales, but sometimes improvising quite new melodies that fitted with the chord changes—very much as jazz soloists do. We know this because composers or performers occasionally wrote out examples of how the music might be performed as a guide for beginners.

Only later did the idea develop that performers should play just what they saw in the score. That is what I was taught to do as an aspiring oboist, and so when I performed trio sonatas I plodded through the notes one after another, wondering why anybody would want to play this stuff.

Knowing and playing

Q: What do you call someone who hangs around with musicians?

A: A viola player.

There is a whole genre of viola jokes, but in the Western classical tradition it is performers in general who have had a bad press—or worse, no press at all. It is an oddly contradictory story. On the one hand the music industry and the media have always focused on star performers from Enrico Caruso and Arturo Toscanini to Luciano Pavarotti and Nicola Benedetti; people go to hear them because it is them, rather than because of what they are performing. On the other hand, historians have traditionally approached music quite differently, focusing on the evolution of style (melodic patterns, harmonic language, rhythm and metre, the relationship between these elements, the formal patterns into which they are cast) and the composers whose 'masterworks'—note the word—are seen as embodying this stylistic evolution.

The result is what by the second half of the 20th century had become the standard format for a one-volume history of music. You began with music's primitive beginnings, perhaps illustrated by examples from Africa or Oceania; then you covered Western music from the medieval period to 1945, focusing on the classical tradition (this was much the longest part). At that point you made some acknowledgement of jazz and American popular music before wrapping up with music in today's increasingly global world. There are a number of problems with this kind of history. It silently prioritizes the West, a term I called problematic because it conflates geography, history, and culture-specific values. Among these values is progress. In this kind of history, music advances inexorably from the past to the present and on towards a future that lies over there, waiting to be revealed: this is a spatialized way of thinking about history that makes whatever happens appear inevitable. It also gives the impression that the term 'Western music' refers to a clearly defined, continuous tradition, rather than a loose assemblage of often local practices only to a limited degree held together by shared instruments, notations, or ideas.

A further problem is that the focus on style turns music into a thing rather than a human practice. While composers—or at least the 'great' composers—were foregrounded in such histories, performers and listeners were in general conspicuously absent. And if performers were mentioned, it was often to be criticized for drawing attention to themselves and so coming between composer and listener, as if they were obstructing the stately progress of music history. Some composers thought the same way: Arnold Schoenberg, one of the pioneers of early 20th-century musical modernism, once remarked that the performer was 'totally unnecessary except as his interpretations make the music understandable to an audience unfortunate enough not to be able to read it in print' (the gendered language was normal at the time). It all added up to a kind of musical class system, an upstairs–downstairs relationship in which the performer's place was below the stairs. Performers were seen as skilled workers whose role was to carry out the tasks assigned to them by the composers who were the real agents of music history. And this had a side-effect. In the classical tradition, women generally played a far greater role in performance than in composition, so they got more or less written out of the history books (and remember that term '*master*works').

In Chapter 3 I will talk about the historical background to this disparagement of classical performers—in reality accomplished artists in a ferociously competitive profession, and the people responsible for everything listeners actually hear. There is one issue I want to address here, however, and it arises from how people learn to perform. Up to the early 19th century, musicians mainly learned their craft by making music with others, often with the help of a teacher or mentor. It was a kind of apprenticeship system, and this kind of learning on the spot can still be found in jazz or popular music (educationalists call it 'informal learning'). But as part of the larger processes of modernization linked to industrialization and urbanization that took place after 1800, learning was relocated to formal institutions of education such as conservatories and universities. Learning through social music-making continued, but as just part of a larger curriculum based on academic knowledge—the kind of knowledge that is codified, set down in textbooks, and taught in classes. By 2000 higher education in music had become part of an institutionalized knowledge industry, a context in which academic research in music thrived.

There is an issue here, and it has to do with the nature of knowledge. The knowledge in terms of which universities operate is based on observation, systematized into generally applicable principles, documented and archived. It is knowledge laid down for the future, a kind of cognitive capital (hence the term 'knowledge economy'). It is what performance students are taught under the title of 'theory', which suggests you become a musician by first learning the theory and then how to apply it in practice. But this is only one kind of knowledge, sometimes called 'explicit' in order to contrast it with the 'tacit' knowledge characteristic of complex decision-making in real time. Think acrobatics, cycling, motor racing, playing videogames, and of course music. This kind of knowledge tends to be embodied rather than purely mental. You recognize it when your fingers know something better than you do.

It is only quite recently that the nature of tacit knowledge and the role it plays in high-level musicianship has been appreciated. This was one reason for the upstairs–downstairs relationship I mentioned. You could see it in musicological conferences, where a theory professor (more often than not male) would analyse some masterwork and a pianist or flautist, often younger and female, illustrated the implications for performance. I am putting this in the past tense because significant progress has been made in addressing this dysfunctional relationship between theory and practice in the culture of classical music. One reason for this is that higher education takes far more notice of other musical traditions than it did just a few decades ago, but even within classical music there are more and more conferences on performance-related topics where academics and performers engage on more equal terms. Serious collaboration between composers and performers is increasingly common too, not least because academic funding regimes favour it.

All the same, it's a bit like gender equality: progress is constantly being made, but the issue doesn't go away. And the most conspicuously successful example of a productive relationship between academic research and performance—between explicit and tacit knowledge—dates back some fifty years to the establishment of historically informed performance, generally abbreviated to HIP. This was the period of the post-war consensus in classical performance style. There was a musical mainstream—a core repertory that roughly went from George Frideric Handel or Johann Sebastian Bach to Claude Debussy or Arnold Schoenberg, depending on your tastes—and within that mainstream all music was played in broadly the same way. There were differences in individual musicians' personal style, to be sure. But the margin of tolerance was quite narrow. Quite *how* narrow becomes obvious if you listen to early recordings, which go back to around 1900 and document the wildly contrasting and sometimes rapidly changing performance styles current during the first half of the century. But until recently few people listened to them.

In saying that in the decades after 1945 all music was played in broadly the same way I mean several things. For one, 18th-century and earlier music was played using modern instruments (pianos instead of harpsichords, modern oboes instead of the very different period instrument). Again, it was performed by large orchestras under a conductor, rather than small ensembles directed from the keyboard by a musician acting as the first among equals; the interpersonal dynamics of performance—the network of cues I described—were different. And much the same kinds of interpretive approach, for example predominantly legato (sustained) tone production and avoidance of excessive speeds, were adopted more or less uniformly across this very varied repertory. Put crudely, this was how music went.

HIP began as a movement to revive 'early'—roughly pre-1700—music, but it was also a reaction against the homogenizing effects of mainstream performance. It was rather like the British Campaign for Real Ale (CAMRA), which dates back to 1971 and was a reaction against the big breweries that had bought up local ones and sold the same tasteless, fizzy product everywhere; campaigners aimed to revive the variety and idiosyncrasy of traditional, hand-made beers. And like CAMRA, HIP was successful. Period-style instruments were reconstructed on the basis of surviving examples or descriptions. But reconstructing period performance techniques and more general principles of interpretation was harder. Even if you played from original notations (rather than the standardized and sometimes bowdlerized editions produced in the 19th and 20th centuries), and putting aside the problem of unnotated ornamentation, notation does not capture the specifics of tone production, dynamics, and articulation (whether notes are joined smoothly or clipped). Consequently the most important source of evidence was period treatises written as a guide for amateur harpsichordists, violinists, flautists, or singers.

But there are problems with these too. Suppose they say that if you see a steady stream of quavers (American eighth notes) you should swing them, as jazz musicians say—that is, make them alternately longer and shorter. But by how much, and does it apply to all genres, instruments, or countries, and within what historical period? Again, if a treatise speaks out strongly against a particular practice, that tells you two things: people did it, and the author didn't like it. So which do you go with? The most intractable problem, however, is that, if notations miss out so much of what a historically informed performer wants to know, words are worse. Say you want to know how much rubato to introduce in your playing (that is, how far to inflect a steady beat). The musicologist Robert Philip, who pioneered the study of early recordings, quotes a co-authored treatise from 1823 that advises the performer to maintain 'an equilibrium between the feelings that hurry him away, and a rigid attention to time'. And Philip comments:

> One can imagine musicians from the eighteenth to the late twentieth centuries nodding their heads in agreement with this carefully worded advice, without having the least idea how much tempo fluctuation the authors really had in mind.

In other words later musicians would read the same words but imagine different performances. Words just do not engage music with anything like the kind of precision that performance—really the musical equivalent of nanoengineering—involves.

To the extent that the problem was solved, it was by bringing together different kinds of knowledge. Music historians familiar with the period literature could collaborate with instrument builders, but performers played an essential role through testing the results, creating a virtuous circle of feedback. The same applies to technique and interpretation: historians tried to make sense of period treatises, struggling with the exasperating vagueness of words about music, while performers would put the historians' interpretations into practice, testing out what worked and what didn't. Often it was only when expert performers tried out what the treatises said that the historians could see what was meant. The contributions of performers were essential to what the historians were doing, and vice versa. Explicit and tacit knowledge worked hand in hand.

Sometimes a single individual was able to bring together these different forms of expertise, but more often it involved collaboration; to this day musicological 'consultants' play a key role in the more research-oriented early music ensembles. And in this way there was a steady development in the performance of early music. The serious-minded but sometimes pedestrian recordings of the 1950s–60s gave way to the panache that David Munrow brought to early music around 1970. Munrow spent his gap year touring South America, bringing back ethnic instruments that he used to perform music going back to the medieval era; he also commissioned copies of obsolete instruments such as racketts and crumhorns. In 1967 he formed the Early Music Consort, an ensemble of about the same size as a typical rock group, and, like a rock group, they toured extensively and made many recordings. By the time of his early death in 1976 Munrow had done more than anyone to build audience enthusiasm for early music, turning it into a movement in the same sense as CAMRA.

And in the following decades HIP gave rise to a new conception of 18th-century music as lighter, fleeter of foot, and more rhetorical than the ponderous style of mainstream performance. A combination of flair and solid professionalism fed into and reflected the development of specialist HIP training at an increasing number of conservatories, especially in Europe. By the end of the century HIP had become an integral part of a broader, more pluralistic mainstream. In orchestral performance there was increased interaction between the HIP and mainstream communities, with lessons learned from HIP being applied to performances using modern instruments; by then the historically informed approach had colonized the core repertory of the Viennese classics (Joseph Haydn, Mozart, and Beethoven), and it has subsequently advanced through the 19th century and into the early 20th. At the same time, a new breed of fortepianists—playing the fortepiano or early form of the piano, a much lighter instrument than the steel-framed behemoth the piano became in the 19th century—was developing a new conception of this repertory that now exists side by side with performances on the modern piano. In this way HIP created quite new and at its best highly appealing music out of old scores.

But this was not achieved without a struggle, and what became known as the 'authenticity' debate raged through the 1980s; scholars, HIP performers, and listeners all took sides. The traditional—or establishment—position was rarely spelled out, but in effect it was that successive developments in instrument design and performance training had brought about huge improvements in standards, and the performance of all music should benefit from them. In contrast the case for authenticity was promoted loudly: you should play music as its composer intended it. This sounds obvious but actually isn't. There is no way you can know what composers intended except through what they wrote—which just takes us back to the problem that notation doesn't capture everything performers need to know.

But there's a more basic issue: *should* we necessarily play music the way its composer intended? The assumption behind the rhetoric of HIP was that there are two ways to play music, right and wrong—and the right way is the historical way. I know of no other performing art in which that is simply taken for granted. In theatre, you can attempt to reconstruct how Shakespeare's plays would have been staged in 1600, but that is just an option: many producers see it as part of their job—and a dimension of their creative freedom—to make them relevant to today's audiences by staging them in new ways (in a New York penthouse, or with gender roles reversed, for example). One of HIP's unfortunate consequences is a historical mindset that closes off such possibilities, and I'll come back to that in Chapter 3.

Eventually Daniel Leech-Wilkinson and Richard Taruskin brought the authenticity debate to a close by arguing that the whole idea of authenticity as historical correctness didn't make sense. In reality, they said, 'historical' performance embodied many of the characteristic qualities of 20th-century modernism, for example the streamlined textures and motor drive of Stravinsky's compositions: it was not undecidable claims of historical correctness but the 20th-century sensibility it embodied that gave HIP its authenticity. At the same time, the undecidability of period style gave historical performers a new freedom of interpretation. In effect, the largely unsupported claims of historical authenticity advanced by early music ideologues operated as a smokescreen behind which newly creative approaches to performance could emerge. And it's striking that HIP's progressive advance through the repertory stopped in the early 20th century—just when the existence of period recordings would have blown away the smoke and enabled the goal of historically correct performance to be actually realized. You can see why that happened. In the age of recording, HIP rhetoric would have turned classical performers into the equivalent of tribute bands and Elvis impersonators.

The key legacy of HIP was to sweep away the basic assumption of the mid-century mainstream that there can be a one-size-fits-all way of playing music. It is not just the recognition that different repertories call for different instruments, techniques, and interpretive styles. It is that whenever and whatever people perform, they have choices, and in making choices they also have responsibilities. They have the freedom and even the obligation to reflect on and interrogate their own practice, and to bring their specialist performer's knowledge to bear upon their personal understanding of the music. And that makes them the co-creators of the music—something that is taken for granted in most other musical cultures, where the upstairs–downstairs relationship between classical composers and performers does not exist.

Music as a political act

Things exist 'out there' in the real world, and the job of language is to represent them—to depict them in the same sense that a painting of a horse depicts a real horse. That is what the philosopher Ludwig Wittgenstein, writing in the 1930s, termed the 'picture' theory of language; it is also called the picture theory of meaning, reflecting the fact that it extends further than just language. In the West there is a tradition of applying the same approach to music too. Seen this way, musical works such as Beethoven's Seventh Symphony exist 'out there' as ideal, timeless entities; they don't cease to exist if the concert hall burns down. And a performance represents or reproduces that ideal entity in real time. In Chapter 3 I shall ask how people came to think this way. But here my aim is to set out a more productive way of thinking about performance.

When he set out this picture theory of meaning, Wittgenstein was not advocating it. On the contrary, he was setting it up as a kind of straw man in order to put forward a quite different model of language and meaning, and at this point he spoke of music. You can understand some language use this way, he said (think of 'the cat sat on the mat'), but you can't think of a musical theme like that. A musical theme is not a sound picture of something: there is no something, no external reality, for it to be a picture *of*. A musical theme is simply what it is. It means what it means. And Wittgenstein's claim is that the same can be true of language.

An obvious example is a promise. When you promise something (e.g. when you say 'I do' during the wedding ceremony), you are not reporting on a state of affairs. Rather you are doing something through the act of saying it. In a term coined by another philosopher, J. L. Austin, this is a performative utterance, meaning it does not simply reflect but actually constructs meaning. And this resonates with another idea that was coming into prominence around the same time. Anthropologists such as Edward Sapir and Benjamin Lee Whorf were working on native American languages, and they found that in some respects they just couldn't be satisfactorily translated into English. The conceptual categories didn't match. Linguistic categories such as tenses or active and passive voices didn't align with English, because in certain fundamental ways native Americans didn't experience the world the same way as English speakers.

Sapir and Whorf's hypothesis was that language determines how people think and experience the world. As with Austin's performative utterances, words do not just reflect how things are but construct meanings. We use words to change things, to *make* things the way they are. And this idea can be applied to art, which in the philosopher Joanna Hodge's words makes available new ways of 'constituting our sense of reality'. Seen this way, she says, Vincent van Gogh created a new way for us to see sunflowers. It's not that we always saw sunflowers like that, but Van Gogh was the first to capture it in paint. It's that we see sunflowers differently because of Van Gogh. And so the significance of painting lies not—or at least not just—in how it represents an external reality, but in how it constructs new forms of perception, understanding, and feeling. This 'constructivist' view of art locates aesthetic value not in the external world but in viewers' experiences. It places viewers at the heart of the aesthetic process. It democratizes art.

So how might such thinking be applied to music? The answer is: in many ways, of which I will give some varied examples. Consider *Frauenliebe und -Leben* (A Woman's Love and Life), a song cycle composed by Robert Schumann in 1840. The texts, by Adelbert von Chamisso, are a narrative of a woman's love for a man, from their first meeting through marriage to his death. Such songs, with piano accompaniment, were often performed in people's homes, and the musicologist Ruth Solie invites us to imagine a young woman performing *Frauenliebe* 'in a small and intimate room...before people who are known to her and some of whom might well be potential suitors'. In such surroundings the distinction between singer and song protagonist blurs, while the woman comes to personify womanhood—and more than that, womanhood as conceived within the patriarchal society of 19th-century Germany. If the woman's future husband is there, her performance may take on the quality of a promise. It will become a performative utterance. Just as with any other promise, the performance does not report on something but *does* something: it creates a changed relationship between the individuals involved.

Of course words are also involved in this example of musical performativity, but in other vocal contexts performative meaning emerges directly from the music. John Potter, a singer whose experience ranges from early music to backing The Who, describes a passage from Antoine Brumel's *Missa Victimae Paschali* in terms of the intimate negotiations and conjunctions between the performers, who are singing one part to each line: 'Throughout, the voices are setting up patterns of tension and relaxation, acutely conscious of each other, both seeking to accommodate each others' desires and to satisfy themselves.' At the end of the first bar, a particular dissonance 'is only a passing moment but it creates a moment of acute pleasure that they may wish to prolong'. As much as a Mozart quartet, the music consists of audible relationships between the parts, which as in *Frauenliebe* blur into the flesh-and-blood individuals performing them. If the words contribute to what Potter describes, it is more for their sound than their sense: it is hardly to the point that they celebrate Easter Sunday. Rather it is Brumel's score that scripts this potential for relational meaning, much as a theatrical script does, and it is the performers who transform the potential into reality.

In other cases—particularly when large choral groups are involved—singing together creates an experience of the individual merging into the collective. A middle-aged Swedish woman recounts something that happened when she was 10:

> We had a school choir, and were rehearsing the end of spring-time assembly.... I remember to this day the bliss I felt when I stood there and sang my part and heard the other voices around me. I could never have imagined such joy. It was as if you left your own body and merged totally with the music.

Accounts of such musical out-of-body experiences are not uncommon: conscious of your own voice but unable to distinguish it from the mass of sound that swirls around you, the sense of merging with the music is equally one of immersion in the community. You feel you belong. These are powerful effects inherent in the very act of collective singing, manifested in sound, and easily harnessed to larger purposes.

Protest songs and national anthems are obvious cases in point. Think of a choir of South African schoolchildren singing the South African national anthem in four-part harmony (Figure 3). It is often referred to as 'Nkosi Sikelel' iAfrica', though properly

3. **Cantare Children's Choir (Gauteng, South Africa), singing the South African national anthem.**

speaking that is the hymn from which the music is taken, and it was sung as an act of defiance under the apartheid regime. Since the end of apartheid, in 1994, this music has resonated with the hopes, the aspirations, and the disappointments of the new South Africa and its sympathizers across the world. But underlying this symbolic and associative meaning is the same sense of solidarity experienced by the Swedish 10-year-old. Through its block-like construction and regular phrasing, the music creates a sense of stability and mutual dependence, with no one of the parts predominating over the others. (Compare the British national anthem, really just a tune plus accompaniment, or the 'Marseillaise', with its individualistic, irregular construction.) It also lies audibly at the interface between European traditions of harmony and African traditions of communal singing, thereby gaining an inclusive quality. Enlisting music's ability to shape individual and group identity, 'Nkosi Sikelel' iAfrica' actively contributed to the creation of what Archbishop Desmond Tutu called the rainbow nation. In such a context, singing is a political act.

And it isn't just singing. Again an example from South Africa makes the point. As the ethnomusicologist Louise Meintjes explains, in the early 1990s studio practices in Johannesburg still bore the impress of apartheid. The engineers, who manipulated the recording equipment and had the technical know-how, were normally white, and their priority was to maximize throughput by avoiding unnecessarily complex technical processes. The producers, in charge of the studio sessions and nominally with overall responsibility for the product, were normally Black—but, being Black, they found it hard to impose their authority on the engineers. At the same time the record companies depended on the producers' inside knowledge of 'local black music styles, languages, audiences, locations, practices, and so forth'. Meintjes's claim is not just that these conflicted relationships were being played out in studios, but that they left their traces in the sound of the records that were made. You could see that as a metaphor for the societal tensions and negotiations through which the new

South Africa was brought into being. But the studio was more than that. It was a metonym, a little bit of South Africa, in which social and political transformation was acted out just as it was elsewhere. And in such a context studio practice, too, becomes a political act.

The same issues arise in orchestral music. The modern orchestra developed more or less in line with the historical process of industrialization and its associated organizational structures. In fact we can describe it in similar terms. It consists of a team of specialists (violinists, oboists, and so on), all working to a pre-existing blueprint or master plan (the score). Within areas of specialism there are teams with identifiable hierarchies and management lines: the leader (lead violinist), first and second violins, first and second oboes, and so forth. In the modern orchestra—as opposed to the 18th-century one—there is also the conductor, who fulfils a specialist management role (he or—sometimes—she does not produce sound as such, but has oversight and responsibility for the whole operation); this is a dedicated career path, with a remuneration package to match. In short, the orchestra embodies organizational structures that characterize modern industrialized society more broadly, and indeed research into how orchestras and other musical ensembles work productively together is an established if peripheral area of management studies.

Note my words. I said the modern orchestra developed in line with industrialization and its associated organizational structures. I didn't say the orchestra—or music more generally—reflects society. That would be like seeing studio recording as a metaphor for South Africa. But again you can think of the orchestra as a part of society within which the same processes are at work, and that way we avoid making an assumption that social change happens elsewhere and is merely reflected in music. Consider: is the move towards smaller, conductorless orchestras such as the Britten Sinfonia a reflection of a broader development towards less hierarchical management styles in industry? Or is it the other way round—that new structures more easily emerge in the performing arts than in commercial contexts policed by the bottom line, and are then taken up elsewhere? If we think of orchestras—and music more generally—as an integral part of society, then change may equally well come from anywhere, a possibility that the idea of music reflecting society rules out of consideration. And that matters, because it means we can see music as an arena in which things can be done that have effects beyond music.

As for Meintjes's idea that the social structures played out in South African studios are inscribed in the music, I can illustrate that too in a classical context. If you play the oboe, you will know that there is a watershed in orchestral writing between Mozart and Beethoven. Mozart's oboe lines make sense in themselves and are gratifying to play; his symphonies are basically scaled up chamber music—music written as much for the players as for audiences. By contrast, Beethoven designs his orchestration from the audience perspective, and as an oboist you may find yourself being patched into first one layer of the orchestral texture and then another, resulting in a line that makes little sense in itself and is less satisfying to play. It all sounds fine when heard from the stalls, but rather than belonging to a musical community the oboist feels like a worker on a musical production line. It's a different social situation. And while I've been describing this in musical terms, it could equally be described in social terms; sound and society are two sides of a single coin. Music does not reflect society but *is* society—society made audible.

Few if any anthropologists today believe in the 'strong' version of the Sapir–Whorf hypothesis, according to which language determines how different cultures experience the world. Rather they believe that language is one of the things that condition cultural experience. In the same way, I am not claiming that musical performance should be understood *only* for what it does as a social or political act rather than as a representation or reproduction of something. Singing 'Nkosi Sikelel' iAfrica' is not just a political act, it is also a performance of the hymn originally composed in 1897 by the Xhosa clergyman Enoch Sontonga; taken up as a liberation song during the period of African decolonization, it was adopted as Zambia's national anthem and then Namibia's, before becoming one of South Africa's two official anthems in 1994. (The other was South Africa's existing national anthem, 'Die Stem van Suid-Afrika', but in 1997 the two anthems were combined into one, with the music coming from 'Nkosi Sikelel' iAfrica'.) Conversely, playing Johannes Brahms's Intermezzo Op. 119 No. 1 is a performance of the work of that name, dating from that final period of Brahms's work in which he retreated into an introspective style suffused with nostalgia and yet in some ways looking forward to the musical future—but then, you might be playing it to your aunt to show what you have achieved in your first term at conservatory and to thank her for putting up the money. In short, musical performances both represent and do things.

Chapter 2
Thinking in music

Music as culture

According to the 13th-century Persian poet and mystic Rumi, 'Love and falling in love can only be explained through love. Reason is totally helpless as its interpreter.' If that is true of love, it is equally true of music. Elvis Costello is one of many people who have said that writing about music is like dancing about architecture, and he added, 'it's a really stupid thing to want to do'. The ethnomusicologist Charles Seeger (father of Pete, the famous folk and protest singer) called this the 'musicological juncture': we want to talk about music, just as we want to share our thoughts and feelings about everything we care about, but as soon as we do so we find it has somehow slipped through our fingers. As with love, though, that doesn't stop people trying.

There is a chronic human urge to put into words things that can't be put into words, but in the case of music it's not just that. It's something built into musical culture itself, something so familiar you take it for granted. Most of the time you make no apparent effort to understand music. You just listen. Like love it can just happen to you, carry you away, charm or enchant or even ravish you. It's as if it was just natural. But of course music isn't natural. It is something we humans make. Music is a cultural product and musicking is a cultural practice. It is artifice, and yet it passes itself off as nature. As the ethnomusicologist Henry Kingsbury puts it, 'the essence of music as a cultural system is both that it is *not* [a] phenomenon of the natural world and also that *it is experienced as though it were*'.

We make and consume music in the here and now—in the moment—but there is more to it than that. When I say music is a cultural product and practice, I mean it exists within a social framework of talking and doing that has a past and that advances into the future. And so music depends on our ability to communicate sounds to one another and to communicate *about* sounds with one another. Yet sounds in themselves—like the feelings they elicit—are transient, slippery, hard to pin down or hold on to: they elude memory, often leaving behind only fleeting impressions, something like waking from a dream. To transform sounds into culture we have to somehow fix them as mental images—to make them tangible, repeatable, communicable. And we do that by turning them into things to make and to hear.

It's not just music. You might say the same of wine or perfume. How do you describe a wine? I pick up a wine catalogue and read at random: an English wine from Blackbook Winery is 'bursting with spice, herb, citrus and grass on the nose with a textured intricate palate'. What sort of a thing is wine that it can have an intricate texture? And how come it is bursting with spice, herb, citrus, and *grass*? Have the makers been adulterating their product? Of course not! The reference to grass is not a literal description: it is a metaphor. It is saying the wine has certain hard-to-describe qualities that it shares with grass (a particular kind of sweetness, perhaps). Winemakers, critics, and catalogues also talk about wine possessing 'fine soft tannins', which is not a metaphor but a scientific term: according to Wikipedia tannins are 'a class of astringent, polyphenolic biomolecules'. In this way, metaphorical and scientific language combine into a hybrid, shared discourse that makes it possible to converse meaningfully about wines. People enjoy talking about wine. There is empirical evidence that the more wine-lovers talk about wines, the more they love them.

All this applies to perfumes too. Jean-Claude Ellena, who creates perfumes for the fashion house Hermès, explains how in the course of their training perfumers acquire a vocabulary of words like soap, aldehyde, jasmine, nail varnish, rose, leather, wood, and bonbon that 'describe the odor and not the object that produces it'. In other words they are metaphorical objects that create 'a mental picture of the odor'. They allow professionals to exchange ideas about how things smell, imagine new combinations of them, and so collaborate in creating the cultural products we call perfumes. This isn't just thinking about scents, it is thinking *in* scents. And while scents are evanescent, no sooner smelled than gone, this shared language builds a community of producers and a culture of production—a culture that, as I put it, has a past and advances towards the future. As cultural products, perfumes have histories.

In the same way music is a culture of sounds, and metaphor is the means by which sound is transformed into the cultural practices of musicking and the cultural products of music. It is almost impossible to talk about music without falling into metaphor of some kind. You might think the movement between one note and another (say an upward leap of a minor sixth) is a real out-there thing, the musical equivalent of a tannin. But on second thoughts it's not so obvious: as the philosopher Roger Scruton asked, 'how can we speak of movement, when nothing moves?' Again, we say this note is higher than that one, but it's not as if high notes come from the sky and deep ones from the earth: it's that they seem lighter or brighter, you might imagine them floating off while low notes settle on the ground—and besides, they are higher on the printed page.

All this falls into the domain of metaphor and hence varies between times and places: in some cultures you don't say one note is higher than another, you say it is bigger. And then there is texture. It's like that wine's textured intricate palate: we readily talk about a piece of music having a particular texture, but what do we mean by it? Bark, moss, velvet, sacking: these things have texture, but how can music when you can't even touch it? If 'textured intricate palate' is a metaphorical way of describing mouthfeel, then does musical texture describe earfeel, and what might that be? And what did you mean by a 'piece' of music? Do you tear strips of music off a roll, like cloth, or chip them off a block? A block of what?

There aren't real-world answers to any of these questions. As with the cultures of wine-making and perfumery, the culture of music involves a system of established metaphors that culture members share—what may be loosely called a language. This is the condition of writing, talking, or thinking about music, but more than that, it is the condition of music's existence as cultural practice and product. It is the dimension of music I'm foregrounding in this chapter, and I'll do so largely by focusing on notations, the most obvious and in some ways culturally significant metaphorical objects within the traditions collectively known—though misleadingly—as Western music. It's true that many musical cultures don't use notations, and those that do may use them very differently. But in one sense or another all musical cultures are based on the construction of sounds as things to make and to hear—whether in terms of physical objects, verbal narratives, or embodied actions—and so the general point I'm making is a much broader one.

Ronald Searle's cartoon summons up a world in which musical sounds leave physical traces rather than just memories (Figure 4). They don't, of course. But in another sense they *do*. We can stockpile recordings or scores, whether as physical objects or in flash memory, and in that form they endure, potentially as long as the world lasts. These are modes of music's existence, just as much as sound is. I can go to an HMV store (though for how much longer?) and buy some music, meaning vinyl or a CD. Or I can buy

'Ruddy music lessons...'

4. Cartoon by Ronald Searle.

it as a download from the iTunes store. If it's classical music I can buy it as sheet music. Then again, if the two of us are listening to something and I say 'I really like this music', I am talking about my experience of it. These things aren't the same, but they are all forms that the music can take; in fact, collectively they *are* the music. And when we write, talk about, or think about music we may have any one of these things specifically in mind, but they are all interconnected, and so any one of them can stand in for the others.

Notation, then, stands in for sound, and it does this by transforming time—the dynamic, situational, and socially produced time I talked about in Chapter 1—into space. There is a story that Stravinsky once pinned the pages of the music he was writing onto the walls of his room, so he could literally walk forwards and backwards through it. You do something similar when you flick through a score, comparing an earlier passage with a later one. The basic principle of Western staff notation is that passing time is represented through a series of marks arranged from left to right on the page. Within the five lines of the staff (or stave), notes are arrayed from high to low. So a score is a kind of two-dimensional plot in which the horizontal axis is time and vertical one is pitch; other than that, just about everything is a conventional symbol of one kind or another. And because paper endures, notation is a means of conservation. It archives music against the failure of individual or social memory. Equally important, it enables communication. The two of us can discuss a piece while we look at the score, with me pointing to a particular passage in order to make some point, and you pointing to some other passage that doesn't fit with what I'm saying.

But these functions of conservation and communication come at a cost. The Argentinian author Jorge Luis Borges wrote a one-paragraph story about a fictitious empire in which, in order to achieve the greatest accuracy, maps were prepared on a 1:1 scale and overlaid on the empire's territory: tattered fragments of them may still be seen in its western deserts, he says. That's absurd, of course, and it would be equally absurd to think of a notation that captured all the detail of musical sounds. Notations work by being highly selective, discarding as much information as possible and retaining only what is necessary for their intended use and users. So what they include and what they miss out depends on the purposes for which they are being used and the knowledge their users bring to them. And this varies widely both within and between cultures.

For example, the neumes first used in Europe over a thousand years ago were aides-mémoires, reinforcing monks' unreliable memories of ecclesiastical chant: they originated in a papal initiative to tighten up the observance of religious ritual. In essence chant is expressively heightened speech, and each neume represents a vocal gesture, sometimes with one neume to a syllable, sometimes with several (Figure 5). In contrast, staff notation—which developed into more or less its modern form by the 17th century—is much more explicit in the detail it provides. Figure 6 is a possible transcription of Figure 5, based on later pitched notations of the chant. It uses noteheads as in conventional staff notation (such as Figure 2), but unlike staff notation it doesn't specify the rhythms: that's because the neumes in Figure 5 don't, and similarly they don't specify particular notes or intervals, just movements up or down. This means that, while neumes work well as an aide-mémoire, you can't sing from them at sight—or at least if you do, you may well sing something quite different from the next person. The additional detail in staff notation enables performers to sight-read music they have never previously seen, so giving rise to quite different ways of using notation. When in the early 18th century Jesuit missionaries introduced the Chinese imperial court to music from the West, it was the ability to play at sight that most impressed the Kangxi emperor.

5. Cantatorium of St Gall (Stiftsbibliothek St Gallen, Cod. Sang. 359), top of p. 150. This manuscript, written on parchment, dates from between 922 and 926, and contains solo chants of the Mass. Neumes are written above the text and keyed to syllables.

But there is a proviso: you can't sight-read just anything, and this has as much to do with you as with the music. Notations omit information on the basis of what the reader is expected to know or to guess. Even where the notation represents every note that is played (and as I explained in Chapter 1 this is often not the case), what you need to know or guess includes practically everything that comes under the heading of performance practice: how fast to perform the music, when and by how much to slow down and speed up, how to articulate the notes, and how to shape the dynamics, along with the countless other decisions that performers make from one moment to the next. These things have a huge impact on how music is experienced by listeners; they can make one performance profoundly moving, another dull or ridiculous or unintelligible, even though the notes are the same. And conventions of performance style have varied massively from one time, place, or genre to another.

Among them are things we take so much for granted that we don't even see them as choices, like how you sing. Nineteenth-century European travellers never tired of comparing Chinese singing to the wailing and yowling of cats, sometimes refusing to accept it as

Al- le- lu- ia.

V. Qui ti- ment do- mi-num

spe-rent in e- um

a- diu- tor et pro- te- ctor

e- o- rum est.

6. Transcription of Figure 5.

music at all. But you don't need to go to another culture to
have such an experience. In 1902 the Gaisberg brothers
(Will and Fred, pioneers of the fledgling recording industry)
travelled to Rome, hoping to record Pope Leo XIII. Leo, then in
his nineties, declined, and instead the Gaisbergs recorded
Alessandro Moreschi, who directed the Sistine Choir and is today
known as the last castrato. There had long been an Italian
tradition of castrating boys with exceptional voices to prevent
them breaking, and the resulting male sopranos took lead roles in
opera as well as in choirs. The practice came to be seen as
barbarous, however, and it was banned in 1861. Castration usually

happened around the age of 8, so Moreschi (born 1858) slipped through the net, and is the only castrato on record.

And what do you hear behind the hiss and crackle of these early recordings? It's hard to describe, but one of its characteristics is an acute, even painful focus of sound, almost like a sublimated primal scream. That is perhaps because he is a castrato (it's hard to know as there aren't other castrati to compare him to), but it isn't just that. There is what might sound like an inability to hit the note properly, but is in fact a kind of grace note: Moreschi attacks notes from an octave or more below the intended pitch, gliding quickly up to it, and combines this with a version of the stylized sob used by Italian operatic tenors at this time. People just don't sing like this now, and if it wasn't for these recordings we wouldn't know they ever did. But it's striking how commentators have resisted this conclusion, looking for one excuse or another not to believe the evidence of their ears: the technology was primitive (but the Gaisbergs also recorded Caruso in 1902, and he sounds great); Moreschi was nervous (he made several recordings in 1902, and more in 1904, and only in the very first one are there audible signs of nervousness); he was too old (he was in his forties); he just wasn't good enough (he was known as 'the angel of Rome', and you didn't just walk into the Sistine Choir).

One reason people resist the evidence of Moreschi's and other early recordings may be that they don't want to believe how much in music isn't captured in scores, the foundational documents of classical music, and consequently how little we actually know about how music sounded before the invention of recording. If someone sang in such an unimaginable way in 1902, then what about 1802 or 1702? Where does that leave the confident claims made by those early music ideologues? There is a sense—a profound sense—in which the history of music up to around 1900 is a history of instruments and scores and treatises and people's accounts of what they heard, but not of music as sound. For that, we have only guesswork—highly informed guesswork, to be sure, but guesswork all the same.

Notations, then, miss out just about everything except the notes, including the knowledge and experience you need to make sense of the notes. As an alternative technology for inscribing music into eternity, recordings (sound or video) present a quite different picture. What you get depends on where you point the microphone or camera, of course, and studio-produced recordings involve other kinds of selection (more on this later). But recording technology is not inherently selective in the way notation is, and that is why—as Moreschi illustrates—it is much better for conserving and transmitting to the future a sense of how music goes. That however is not the only purpose served by the representation of music. Within the Western classical tradition notations have served another and in some ways more vital purpose. They are one of two key ways in which musicians think not only about music but *in* music. And in that context selection is everything.

Writing it to hear it

If notation is one of the key ways in which musicians think in music, the other is instruments. The same principles apply to both, but they are easier to explain in relation to instruments, so I will start there and come back to notations. What instrument you play can affect how you think about music and even how you hear it. If you play the oboe you are led to think of music as a single, continuously nuanced stream of sound, shaped from microsecond to microsecond by the intimate physical engagement of lips and reed, and monitored by ear; for a pianist, by contrast, 88 separate keys lie ready at hand. The oboist's single stream of sound means each note is transformed into the next, whereas the piano's 88 keys activate 88 separate sound-producing mechanisms. That means it's easy for pianists to create permutational patterns such as broken-chord accompaniments (you keep your hand still and just move your fingers): what is harder is to create the effect of a single continuous line, what pianists call making the piano sing.

There is more to it. The piano keyboard is made up of a pattern of white keys punctuated by two black keys (C#, D#) and then three more (F#, G#, A#), which is repeated in octaves. So you make the same movements to play a pattern of notes an octave higher—you just shift your hand to the right—and likewise what you hear is the same pattern, only an octave higher. In other words the pattern on the keyboard maps onto the pattern of the sounds. This means if you internalize the spatial layout of the keyboard, you have a mental scheme that will accommodate the sounds. To some extent all this applies to the oboe too: in principle fingerings repeat at the octave, but the modern instrument has a great deal of metal keywork added to make it easier to play particular notes or transitions between notes, and this complicates things. And at the top of the instrument's register the fingering patterns become complex and unpredictable, so the mapping between instrument and sound fizzles out. Because of these complications and because it can only produce a single stream of sound, the oboe is not generally as good for thinking with as the piano. Historically most Western composers have been keyboard players.

People think with instruments in the same sense that Chinese shopkeepers traditionally did sums with an abacus (some still do), but it's not just the instrument that is involved: it's the relationship between the instrument and the musician's body. Fingers and keys operate as a coupled system grounded in physical engagement. And sound is part of this. David Sudnow, a sociologist who learned to play jazz piano as an adult and documented his learning process, writes that in the flow of improvisation

> the piano is no longer experienced as an external mass of ivory and
> wood and steel, but...seems to dissolve into an inner acquisition of

spaces to speak with. Keys are no longer encountered as places having lower limits that speak back to the hand as physical boundaries, but as places having sounds throughout their depths.

In other words, sound becomes a dimension of the engagement of body and instrument. Fingers, keys, and sound form a single networked system.

You can understand this in terms of what philosopher Andy Clark calls the 'extended mind'. Think of Scrabble: you shuffle the letter tiles on your rack, looking for words you can form with them (and how to get rid of that pesky Q). Rearranging the tiles helps you think of the words. It's the same as using pencil and paper, or in days long past a slide rule, to work something out. In each case, you are thinking with physical objects; the objects are an integral part of your thinking. As Clark says, if 'a part of the world functions as a process which, *were it done in the head*, we would have no hesitation in recognizing as part of the cognitive process, then that part of the world *is* . . . a part of the cognitive process'. You can see how this relates to musical instruments. If fingers, keys, and sound form a single networked system, then for an experienced pianist each of these dimensions can stand in for the others. Even if there is no instrument and no sound—even if the pianist is just feeling the music in her fingers—the same cognitive circuits and processes are activated. That is how instruments enable you to think in music.

So how might all this translate to notation? We need to begin by drawing a distinction. There are many different notations for music, and one class of them is tablatures (guitar tablature is the most common, but tablatures are found across many cultures). Put simply, tablatures tell you what to do. The very earliest tablature for the Chinese long zither or *qin* (Figure 7) consisted of prose instructions: put your finger on that string, press down here, and pluck like this. More modern tablatures consist of symbols. Guitar tablature uses six lines because the standard guitar has six

7. Zha Fuxi (1895–1976) playing the *qin*.

strings, and the tablature is a schematic picture of the instrument. For each string there are figures that tell you where to put your finger on the fretboard (0 means an open string, 1 the first fret, and so on). The great advantage of guitar tablature is that it is easy to learn: do what it says and the right notes will come out. The disadvantage is that it only works for guitars: because each instrument is different, every tablature is different. In contrast staff notation works for any instrument, because instead of being a schematic picture of the instrument, it is a schematic picture of the sound.

But it is a picture based on particular assumptions about the nature of the sound. I can make the point in terms of another system of musical representation: MIDI (Musical Instrument Digital Interface) code, invented in 1982 so that synthesizers and other gear made by different manufacturers could talk to one another (up to then manufacturers each used their own, incompatible codes). Because of its limited purpose—MIDI was designed with keyboard-based pop in mind—the code basically treats all music as keyboard music, with a set of separate sound producers that can be individually switched on or off. Consequently it has a lot of trouble handling glissandos or other kinds of continuous change between one note and another. Staff notation works on the same basic assumption as MIDI code, that all music is made up of discrete entities called notes—the musical equivalent of atoms, each corresponding to a single key and represented by a notehead. But in reality not all music is made up of discrete entities of this kind. The highly ornamented style of South Indian singing, for example, is continuously shaped and inflected; the voice passes through various pitches (C, C♯, D) in the same sense that a graphline passes through various numerical values (1.0, 1.5, 2.0), but it's not a series of separate notes like beads on a string. And the same applies to a greater or lesser degree to all singing, as well as to jazz saxophone performance, for example. It's in that sense that, unlike atoms, notes have a metaphorical rather than an objective existence. As I said, they are metaphorical objects.

Notations, then, are tied up with larger musical values, and again the *qin* makes the point. In modern *qin* tablature, customized characters specify how you should pluck the note, and there is an extraordinarily large number—conventionally twenty-six—of these. (Whether that really amounts to twenty-six aurally distinguishable sounds is doubtful, and not entirely relevant, since *qin* players value the choreography of hand movements as well as the sound.) On the other hand, like the neumes of medieval chant, *qin* tablature does not show rhythms at all; at most, a little circle may be inserted between musical phrases. It would hardly be possible to imagine anything more different from staff notation, with its elaborate specification of rhythm but almost complete disregard of articulation, timbre, and vibrato, the dimensions of sound implicated in the twenty-six ways of plucking the *qin*.

But of course that doesn't mean that articulation, timbre, and vibrato don't matter in classical performance, or that rhythm is of no concern to *qin* players and their listeners. It means each system specifies just what is necessary for the notation's intended use. In the Western context that means performance from notation, often by ensembles, of an extensive and mainly unmemorized repertory (so playing at sight matters). In the Chinese context, it means prolonged private study of a small repertory of solo pieces, memorized and played in an often highly personal manner (so sight-reading is irrelevant and issues of coordination don't arise). These are very different contexts of use, but in either case performers supply the information that is absent in the notation. And that means it's wrong to think of notations as if they captured everything we care about in music. As neumes illustrate, notations support and supplement, but do not substitute for, memory and stylistic knowledge. For performers they they are certainly not a substitute for listening. That is why I said in Chapter 1 that, even when they have the printed music in front of them, performers are playing by ear.

And if notation supports and supplements memory and stylistic knowledge for performers, it can also serve as an environment for what might be called what-if simulation, in other words for imagining music that does not (yet) exist. Jeanne Bamberger, a piano prodigy turned psychologist and educationalist, writes that notations and the terminology that goes with them give us 'the power to play with the things named, shifting our attention at will among them and combining them in novel ways'. For an illustration, look again at Figure 5. As I said, each neume represents a vocal gesture. You can substitute one gesture for another, but beyond that the notation doesn't help you play with the music. In contrast, look again at Figure 6. Here the neumes often correspond to several individual noteheads (look for example at the beginning of the second line). The transcription fragments each neume into separate atoms of pitch and time that can be manipulated independently. Each note represents a separate decision point, a point where you could do something else.

In this way staff notation—which combines noteheads with further symbols to specify rhythmic and other features—invites play. How would it be if you changed this note for that one, inverted the melodic profile of these notes or put them the other way round, extended this note by interpolating these other notes? What if you exported this rhythmic profile to that series of pitches, or vice versa? We are moving towards recognized compositional techniques (the last sentence describes rhythmic and melodic motives). I could plod on through progressively more complex examples that increasingly resemble real-world composition. But instead I'll make a leap: to Bryn Harrison, a contemporary British composer known for complex rhythmic notations. Harrison cites Jasper Johns, the godfather of pop art, who once said 'Sometimes I see it and then paint it. Other times I paint it and then see it.' (It's the same idea as Joanna Hodge on Van Gogh's sunflowers.) And Harrison riffs on this: in his music, he says, 'I'm writing it to hear it, as much as I'm hearing it to write it.' In other words notation leads him to discover new things to hear. You might compare his scores to maps that chart hitherto undiscovered territories of sound, revealing things that nobody knew were there to be heard.

As I said at the beginning of this chapter, music is slippery, no sooner heard than gone. Instruments and notations are devices through which you can get a grip on it, retain it in mind, and manipulate it through what-if simulations; for an experienced musician, imagery derived from instruments and notations is part of a cognitive network that also includes sound. At one time—less so today—there was a premium on the ability to 'hear' sound in your head, and so musicians would make exaggerated claims that they could imagine music just as clearly as hearing it in real life, if not more so. There was an idea that composers could 'hear' sounds in their heads and then just write them out, as if by dictation. That was one of many 19th-century myths about classical music I shall talk about in Chapter 3. It suggests a very passive idea of how you create music, as if all you have to do is press a 'Play' button in your brain. In reality creating music is something much more active, by which I mean both proactive and interactive.

One way to put it is that you work with real or imagined sounds and—in Sudnow's phrase—let them speak back to you. I can illustrate this through a piece for solo guitar, *Forlorn Hope*, on which the British composer David Gorton collaborated with the guitarist Stefan Östersjö. Östersjö was using an eleven-string alto instrument, and Gorton had devised a number of customized tuning systems for it. Gorton and Östersjö worked together over two days, Östersjö experimenting and improvising, Gorton listening and sometimes making comments or suggestions. There was one six-minute episode during which, trying a new tuning, Östersjö almost immediately hit on an intriguing chordal pattern. He then played with it uninterrupted for several minutes, ending with a bell-like harmonic plucked above the fingerboard: Gorton leant forward and asked what that was. Much of the final piece drew directly from this six-minute episode, developing and exploring the various things that had happened during it. This, then, is an example of interacting with the instrument. The guitar did things neither Gorton nor Östersjö anticipated. It spoke back to them.

And there is the same kind of interaction in the way composers work with notations. Sometimes they invent private rule-based systems that govern the notes you can use in some particular context, the order in which they come, and so forth. David Lang, for example, talks about how at an early stage of his career he would set up 'ridiculous rules' to see what he could do within them, while song-writing manuals sometimes suggest giving yourself arbitrary constraints to stimulate your imagination. Some experienced composers do it too. The Pulitzer Prize-winning American composer Roger Reynolds spends a lot of time working out complicated mathematical systems and structures—where numbers translate into notes—before he starts composing his music in the sense of writing out what the performers will play.

If notations really captured everything that matters in music, you might be able to set up notation-based rules to automate musical decision-making. But that's not what Reynolds is doing. He isn't just turning the handle and churning out the music. Instead, he insists, the point is to create a kind of musical environment or workspace that will release his moment-to-moment creativity in the act of composition: he calls it 'the freeing of local invention for more intuitional vibrancy'. His apparently over-rationalized procedure gives concrete form to compositional problems that stimulate him to improvise solutions, suddenly seeing (hearing) what he wants. And the result of this process, he says, is an otherwise unachievable spontaneity. Brian Ferneyhough, the leading 'New Complexity' composer, explains his use of computer software along the same lines.

The music laboratory

How might these various aspects of creative imagination in music work together in practice? A concrete example is provided by Beethoven, whose compositional process became central to a whole way of thinking about classical music that lasted well into the 20th century and even now has not entirely disappeared. This didn't happen just because Beethoven was widely seen as the greatest composer that had ever been. It was also because he sketched much more than most composers, and—just as important—did not throw away his sketches. Even better, he used pre-bound sketchbooks, normally starting each book at the beginning and working through to the end. In the years after Beethoven died many of the sketchbooks were divided up and the fragments scattered across the world. But a major post-war musicological effort tracked down these fragments and reconstructed the original form of the sketchbooks, and as a result it is possible to follow in unusual detail how Beethoven composed.

In 1814 he started work on what would have been his Sixth Piano Concerto, making about seventy pages of sketches for the first movement and starting on a full score (a score that includes all the instruments of the orchestra) before abandoning the project. Back in the late 1980s I was involved in the creation of a performing edition of the score as Beethoven may have envisaged it, so I will use that as my example. As with the conventional song structures of pop, there were more or less set patterns into which classical music fell, and this movement was conceived as the concerto variant of sonata form. The detail doesn't matter for now; the point is that the sections of that form provided the framework for Beethoven's sketching. Within each section he worked initially on the thematic materials (pithy melodic ideas designed to be developed into a kind of musical argument), and then on the passages connecting them. After that he pulled together these various materials into a continuous draft, before moving on to the next section and repeating the process.

This was followed by a phase in which, instead of sticking to the chronological progression of the movement, Beethoven tried out the themes in different contexts, figuring out how he would be able to use them in those parts of the movement he had not yet sketched. After that there was a phase of trouble-shooting, in which he jumped around to various unclear or problematic parts of the emerging movement. Only now was he ready to embark on a series of increasingly lengthy drafts that brought together everything he had sketched so far. This was the point when he started on the full score—earlier in the process than usual, and apparently too early, as the score starts confidently but becomes increasingly sketchy as it continues, with crossings-out multiplying (and sometimes nothing being written in their place). Beethoven must have thought he was closer to settling the music in his mind than he really was, and it's interesting to see him miscalculating over this. It could have something to do with why he abandoned the movement, but more likely the reason was he

8. Beethoven's Mendelssohn 6 sketchbook, p. 114. This sketchbook, which Beethoven used during 1814, is now located at the Biblioteka Jagiellońska, Kraków.

had intended to play the solo part, and now realized his increasing deafness made this unrealistic.

The sketches are generally in one or two staves. Figure 8 shows the earliest page associated with the concerto; the first line is what turned into the second main theme, the third a long trilled A that is the piano's first entry. Beethoven is writing fast and for his eyes only, so he doesn't bother with clefs, key signatures, or sometimes accidentals—which means you can't always be completely sure what pitches the noteheads represent. Sometimes it isn't even clear which end of the penstroke is meant to be the notehead, so you have to decide what makes most sense in context. In general, as here, he focuses on the top line of the texture; most of the time you can deduce the harmonies he had in mind, though occasionally he would add something to clarify them. But the most striking thing about the sketches is how iterative the process is. He sketches the same passages again and again. It is as if the very act of writing prompted mutations that sometimes enabled Beethoven to see where he wanted to go—and sometimes not, resulting in a change of tack.

When I spoke of the 'act' of writing I was referring to something more than marks on paper. As you look at them you become conscious of the physicality of the process as Beethoven pushes the notes around and—again in Sudnow's phrase—they speak back to him. He is thinking in music, but he is thinking on paper. And the sketches aren't just a record of his thinking: in a sense, they *are* his thinking. It's like something the American theoretical physicist Richard Feynman said to historian of science Charles Wiener, who was interviewing him about his working methods. Wiener referred to one of Feynman's working notes as a record of what he had done in his head, and Feynman picked him up: 'No, it's not a *record*', he said. 'It's *working*. You have to work on paper and this is the paper. Okay?' In the same way Beethoven worked on paper and that is one of the ways he thought in music. It's another illustration of Clark's extended mind.

When you speak of Beethoven's compositional process everyone thinks of his sketches, but they are just part of the story—the part that survives. What doesn't survive is what Beethoven did at the piano. Another of those 19th-century myths is that *real* composers don't work at the piano (they do everything in their heads). Luckily nobody told Beethoven. When in 1823 he gave Archduke Rudolph advice on composing, Beethoven recommended he keep a small table next to his piano so as to move easily from one to the other, and there are contemporary accounts of how when composing Beethoven would repeat the same thing over and over again at the piano—just as he did on paper. When you work through his sketchbooks you sometimes see gaps where Beethoven's conception of what he was after was suddenly transformed—and these most likely mark points where he moved over to the piano. You also see sketches that look quite well worked out but oddly truncated, which I take to be things Beethoven had come up with at the keyboard and jotted down before he forgot them.

If one of Beethoven's creative techniques was doing things again and again, another was changing perspective. The most obvious example is the quite different perspectives of sketchbook and piano, but even within the sketches you can see him alternating between detailed work and a zoomed-out view (such as those extended drafts I referred to). Each perspective provides a partial image of the emerging music, so that the combination of them yields a more complete conception of it, while the transition between one perspective and another may spark new ideas. And whereas the sketchbooks I have been talking about are large-format 'desk' ones (the large format allows you to see as much as possible at once), there are also 'pocket' sketchbooks that Beethoven took with him when he went out; he was known for his walks in the Vienna woods, and there is a contemporary account of how he frequently 'stopped, with a sheet of music paper and a pencil stump in his hands, as if listening, looked up and down and then scribbled notes on the paper'. That is an example of changing perspective in the most literal sense—and one that many creative practitioners find helpful when they have something to work out.

When we put all this together it gives us a picture of what we might call Beethoven's compositional ecology. Piano and sketchbook afforded complementary but interconnected ways of thinking in music, each prompting new ideas or ways of developing existing ones; at the same time both confronted these ideas with some kind of empirical reality (sounding or looking right or wrong). Brian Eno has drawn a contrast between the empirical nature of studio composition, where you are literally working with sound, and the abstract nature of score-based composition, where you are working with symbols only later turned into sound. But that's not quite right, and not just because—contrary to the myths—classical composers worked at the keyboard. Instrument, notation, the playing or writing body, and sound together made up the multi-modal, networked system through which they thought in music, and through which the emerging composition talked back to them. It was at work whether they were at the keyboard, at a desk, or in the woods. And that explains one of the classic conundrums about Beethoven. How was he was able to compose some of his most famous works after he had become stone deaf? Perhaps the answer is obvious. Even if he could no longer hear physical sound, the network—the mental structure of which sound was an integral part—remained in place. He was still composing by ear, even though he heard nothing.

Yet another 19th-century myth was that great composers somehow conceived their music all at once, in a flash of inspiration, so that they merely had to write down what was already formed in their heads. Clearly whoever thought up that never looked at a Beethoven sketchbook. It is not just that Beethoven wrote down tiny scraps of melody he thought of in the woods for fear of forgetting them before he got home. It is the way you see him labouring to make something of initial ideas that could have come to him in the woods or at the keyboard, or even while doodling on paper, following his pen to see where it took him. The process is laborious—convoluted, sometimes full of false turns, though at other times proceeding swiftly to a conclusion—because Beethoven did not know where it was going to end up. That, of course, is the point of sketching.

The French philosopher Maurice Merleau-Ponty once compared writing to weaving: you work on the wrong side of the fabric, he said, and suddenly find yourself surrounded by meaning. But it is true of music too, and Merleau-Ponty's image embodies two key points I want to make. The first is that composition is a process through which music emerges in the very act of composing, of searching for a goal as yet unknown. The second is that there are two sides to the musical fabric, two fundamental dimensions of music's existence. There is music as experienced in the dynamic, situational, socially produced time of performing and listening—music heard so easily, so effortlessly, that it seems to be given in nature. That is what most people mean when they speak of 'music'. But there is also the other side of music, where it is laboriously stitched together—a process that takes place in a quite different (and more extended) time and involves specialist knowledge and techniques. It is because there are two sides to the musical fabric that music is the artifice that passes itself off as nature.

Chapter 3
The presence of the past

Express yourself

In this chapter I trace a number of key ideas going back to the
18th century that still condition music and thinking about it in the
West today, though the values underlying them have often changed.
Here I am largely talking about classical music and a little
explanation is in order. The term 'classical' (small-C) music refers
to the more or less elite Western traditions of notated music,
though there is not a clear distinction between these and more
popular traditions that range from light music and dance music to
parlour songs and hymns. In terms of chronology it is not a very
specific term, whereas 'Classical' (big-C) music refers to a
particular series of developments centred on Vienna and the
Austro-Hungarian Empire during the late 18th and early 19th
centuries—developments in which the trio of Haydn, Mozart, and
Beethoven played a key role. In retrospect this came to be seen as
a golden age, a permanent standard of artistic achievement; the
art and literature of Classical Greece and Rome were seen the
same way, and that is where the term 'Classical' comes from. That
is the focus of the main part of the chapter, but in the last part I
trace the beginnings of a very different, you might say post-classical
idea of what music is and what it is for—an idea that came fully
to fruition only with the development of digital technology.

Around 1750, classical music might be divided into three loose categories: the primarily choral, generally self-contained, and sometimes archaic musical culture of the church; the instrumental music associated with royal and aristocratic courts, typically elegant and based on the dances that played a prominent role in high society; and opera, which took place partly at the courts but also—particularly in Italy and England—in commercial opera houses. Music found its most prestigious place in opera, a primarily theatrical genre which—like the painting of the time—dealt principally with classical, mythological, or historical subjects. The music set the stage but its key role was in characterization. Opera of this period combined recitative—a kind of heightened speech with light musical accompaniment that moved the plot on—with arias generally sung by just one of the stage characters, where the action stopped and the dramatic and emotional situation was explored. Music was central to this, and involved representation in two different senses. First, the music represented the stage character and his or her state of mind. Second, it did this according to a kind of lexicon of emotions, each represented by a more or less conventionalized musical expression.

Leading musicians of the late 18th century, including Haydn and Mozart, were often both operatic and instrumental composers, and they brought an operatic conception to instrumental music—to keyboard music, string quartets, and orchestral works. Some of Mozart's keyboard sonatas, written for the recently invented piano, create a sonic equivalent of operatic stage sets. Just as there was a musical lexicon of emotions in opera, so there was a lexicon of so called 'topics' in instrumental music: characteristic musical materials associated with particular real-world contexts such as the church (represented by archaic counterpoint), the concert hall (represented by virtuoso figuration), or the hunt (represented by conventional patterns of horn calls). The result is that what looks in the score like just piano music could be heard, in Wye Jamison Allanbrook's words, as 'a miniature theater of human gestures and actions'.

I'll come back to that, but more consequential is the way the operatic language of character representation was translated into a new style of instrumental music. Here the best illustration is the string quartet. The complex interactions between players that Arnold Steinhardt talked about are also interactions between virtual characters played by the instruments, and here 'play' takes on a sense of role play. An early biography of Haydn characterizes one of his quartets as consisting of an affable, middle-aged man (first violin), his friend who is more retiring and tends to agree with everyone else (second violin), and a solid, well-read citizen (cello). The viola, in the tradition of viola jokes, is 'a somewhat loquacious matron' who really has nothing to say but insists on saying it all the same. This is a frankly humorous description, and in any case instruments often change characters every few bars in Haydn's and Mozart's quartets, but the basic idea is on the money. It was something of a cliché to compare the genre of string quartet to civilized conversation among friends.

The same language of character and emotion was found in the less intimate, more public, and more formal genre of symphonic music. A common pattern (the sonata form I referred to in Chapter 2) involved two groups of thematic materials with contrasted characteristics and in different keys, worked together in the course of a movement to reach some kind of agreement or reconciliation. This instrumental drama differs from opera in being based round abstract musical agents rather than staged individuals, and that gives it greater fluidity. As in string quartets, instrumental characters morph into one another or enter into kaleidoscopically changing relationships, in a way you don't see on the operatic stage or indeed in real life. It's a world in which human qualities and relationships exist in a condensed and intensified form—in some ways like the role play you find in virtual worlds such as Second Life, which (as digital anthropologist Tom

Boellstorff says) 'draw upon many elements of actual-world sociality' but reconfigure them in contrafactual ways.

The responses of some contemporary listeners and critics underline this. In 1769 the German critic Gotthold Ephraim Lessing wrote, 'Now we melt with sympathy and suddenly we are to rage,' and asked, 'Why? How? Against whom? Against the person for whom our soul just now was all pity? or someone else?' Measuring the new instrumental conception against the norms of opera or everyday life, Lessing was bewildered by the rapid succession of contradictory, apparently ungrounded feelings. Nevertheless the urge he expresses to hear the music as representing character persisted, and by the turn of the 19th century listeners and critics were increasingly hearing Beethoven's symphonies as character studies, portraits in sound of some exceptional individual. This is something that Beethoven himself encouraged when he named his Third ('Eroica') Symphony after Napoleon Bonaparte. And though he tore up his inscription on realizing that Bonaparte was just another dictator, he replaced it with a title that elicited exactly this kind of interpretation: 'Heroic symphony, composed to celebrate the memory of a great man'.

We can trace the evolution of this way of hearing Beethoven's music through critical responses to his Ninth Symphony. A report of its premiere, in 1824, picks up on the idea of heroism but applies it to Beethoven himself: 'the public received the musical hero with the utmost respect and sympathy'. Another early review describes the music in terms of a heroic scenario in which Beethoven is the protagonist: 'Beethoven's power of imagination tears the earth asunder when it tries to check his fiery progress' (and much more in this vein). The music does not just depict struggle, it is Beethoven's struggle. A review from 1828 takes this a stage further: now it is Beethoven's struggle with deafness, and the symphony as a whole represents his path from suffering to joy. The music is not just by but *about* Beethoven. And a further review explains the genre-bending introduction of voices in the

final movement as necessary 'so that he may express himself
adequately. How will he express himself? What shall be his song?
What else but a song of Joy!'

At this point, the story links up with changes in concert culture
that had been taking place throughout this period. As rural
populations migrated to cities and a newly leisured bourgeoisie
developed, symphonic music spread from royal or aristocratic
courts to public concerts. And linked to this was a change in
practices of listening. Opera houses were designed for social
listening: the design of boxes reflected this, encouraging people to
socialize as much as watch the stage. In the new symphonic
concerts everybody faced the stage, and a newly serious style of
listening developed in which you aimed to absorb the music into
the core of your subjective being. Figure 9 makes the point. The
title tells us that the seven men are at a concert, though we don't
see the hall. Each seems to be hearing the music quite differently
(though at least one appears to have dozed off); there is no more
contact between them than there is between earbudded travellers
in a subway train. Each is wrapped up in a world of his own, as if
Beethoven's music is addressing him individually, speaking
confidentially to him and to him alone. It is an experience of
vicarious intimacy.

The trend continued. Six years after Lami's painting, in 1846,
Richard Wagner—later a hugely influential composer of opera, or
in his preferred term music drama—described the Ninth Symphony
as Beethoven's attempt to reach out from the solitude of his
deafness: 'When you meet the poor man, who cries to you so
longingly', he wrote, 'will you pass him on the other side if you find
you do not understand his speech at once?' Engagement with
Beethoven's music meant a commitment to Beethoven himself, or
at least to the idealized image of Beethoven purveyed by a flood
of hagiographic biographies and adulatory programme notes.
As the Beethoven cult continued into the 20th century, the French
writer Romain Rolland held up Beethoven as a role model for the

9. Eugène Lami, *The* Andante *from the Symphony in A*. This watercolour dates from 1840 and its present whereabouts are unknown. This title is the artist's own, visible at the bottom left and referring to Beethoven's Seventh Symphony, but the painting is more commonly referred to as *Upon Hearing a Beethoven Symphony*.

modern age, epitomizing personal sincerity, altruism, and self-denial; he virtually reduced Beethoven to a single motto, 'Joy through suffering'—actually a wry comment in one of Beethoven's letters about the tribulations of travelling in Croatia, but transformed by Rolland into a universal ethical principle. And this idea was extended beyond Beethoven to other composers (including Wagner). Classical music became a fan culture.

There is nothing to say music has to be heard this way. As the musicologist and psychologist Robert Gjerdingen puts it, in the 18th century the idea that music was about its composer's feelings would have seemed as outlandish as the idea that a chef's tart sauce was about his tartness (actually not so far from the way today's *MasterChef* contestants insist their signature dishes express their personality). And by the beginning of the 20th century, this kind of composer-based fan culture had largely died down in classical music. There were superstar classical performers, especially after the development of recordings: Caruso is an outstanding example. But increasingly it was popular music, now developing through recording into a huge international industry, that lay at the centre of fan culture. Think of the crooners from the decades after 1930, singers such as Bing Crosby and Frank Sinatra. They were so called because they developed a way of singing made possible by the invention of the microphone. Whereas Western classical vocalization had developed to fill increasingly large venues, the crooners were able to adopt a softer, more lifelike style, singing close to the microphone: it was as if they were singing directly in your ear, again addressing you personally and confidentially.

Fan culture became even more intense in the post-war era of Elvis and the Beatles. But what I want to emphasize is how the originally classical idea of music as self-expression became associated with a host of solo artists such as (choosing names more or less at random) Bob Dylan, Neil Young, or David Bowie. As performers and songwriters, they were working (as Dylan and Young still are) within a culture in which the classical distinction of composer and performer was not salient: they were seen as authors, the primary agents of their music. As with Beethoven, engagement with their music entailed a personal commitment to them, or at least to the idealized image of them constructed through magazine articles, liner notes, and television programmes. And again as with Beethoven, the core of fandom lay in the sense of vicarious intimacy between artist and listener.

A further link between the classical tradition and 20th-century popular music follows from this. If music was the composer's self-expression, then composers had to be true to themselves. Sincerity was the foundation of Rolland's Beethoven cult. The worst crime composers could commit was to sell out—to betray their personal style and aesthetic values in order to court popularity, worldly success, money. Even Beethoven was not beyond suspicion. At the time of the Congress of Vienna (1814–15), when the European powers came together to negotiate a new world order after the Napoleonic wars, Beethoven wrote what were later condemned as a series of pot-boilers; the most successful was *Wellingtons Sieg* (Wellington's Victory), a cine-realistic depiction of the Battle of Vitoria complete with spatial effects and imitation gunfire. The judgement of Beethoven's celebrated biographer Maynard Solomon is typical: 'the unaccustomed popular acclaim and financial reward reaped by *Wellington's Victory* tempted him to mine this vein for all it was worth', and the works of this time are 'the nadir of Beethoven's artistic career'.

In the last decades of the 20th century such thinking still remained powerful. If Beethoven was not beyond suspicion, neither was Dylan. When in 1966 Dylan played at the Free Trade Hall, Manchester, an audience member shouted out 'Judas!' Ostensibly it was because Dylan had abandoned his acoustic guitar for an electric one; symbolically the heckler was accusing him of betraying the tradition of protest music. (According to another fan, 'it was like, as if, everything that we held dear had been betrayed...We made him and he betrayed the cause'.) Either way, Dylan had sold out. It is the same issue of personal authenticity we saw in the Prudential commercial with which I began this book, which turned on how the protagonist could be true to himself—could be the musician he aspired to be—but at the same time provide for his old age. And it applied to bands as much as to individuals. It is part of the definition of rock bands that they create their own music. Those that do not—or worse, that are artificially put together by entrepreneurs—are seen as inauthentic; hence the critical opprobrium heaped on the Monkees. Again, proper rock bands (think Rush) can cut it on stage. They don't depend on technological wizardry to cover up their lack of natural musicianship; hence the criticism of the

American singer Ashlee Simpson in 2004, when a technical glitch revealed that she was lip-synching to a recorded track during a supposedly live performance.

The idea of authenticity was not just used as a weapon against the manufactured bands, lip-synching, and other forms of artifice in popular culture. It could also be used as a stick with which to beat classical music (ironically, considering that it had come from there in the first place). The point is made by an episode of the children's television series *The Ghost of Faffner Hall*, a spin-off from Jim Henson's Muppets that aired in 1989. It features Piganini, a virtuoso musician of the European tradition, whom the janitor finds hiding in a broom cupboard (Figure 10). Despite his prodigious technique, the porcine celebrity has a fatal flaw: he can only play scales, and even then, only if he has the music in front of him. But as he tells the janitor, his audiences demand that he plays the little black notes in all sorts of different sequences, 'all piggley-higgley', and this has brought on a crisis of confidence. Luckily the janitor turns out to be the famous blues, folk, and country musician Ry Cooder. He pulls out his guitar and gives Piganini a quick lesson in what it means to improvise, to play from the heart, to play real music—which, it turns out, sounds remarkably like the blues. Of all the genres of popular music, this is the one most closely associated with the heartfelt self-expression of oppressed peoples in the American Deep South. A complex national and racial dynamic is at work in this brief encounter between American popular culture and the European classical tradition.

Here then the contrast between authenticity and inauthenticity is figured as the contrast between nature and artifice. It is a way of thinking built on an idea of music as self-expression that came into place in the early 19th century and remains part of today's musical environment. The past lives on in the present, even when the values informing it change.

10. Still from *The Ghost of Faffner Hall* (1989), showing Piganini and Ry Cooder.

Monuments in sound

If the story I told in the previous section started with the operatic representation of character, then ideas of music as representation also developed in a quite different way during the 19th century. This is where I come back to the idea of musical works such as Beethoven's Seventh Symphony existing 'out there' as ideal, timeless entities represented or reproduced in performance. How might people have come to think that way?

Actually there is a long tradition of such thinking. It goes back at least as far as the ancient Greek philosopher Plato, and was current in the early medieval period, when people began to think of neumes—introduced, as I said, as a practical aide-mémoire—as the earthly reflection of a higher order of being. During the Italian Renaissance the idea developed of artistic genius, the term implying access to that higher order of being: the artist was a mediator, a channel through whom supramundane realities and revelations were translated into human culture. By the 18th century, inspired artists were widely seen as working at a level that transcended conceptual understanding, even their own. And all these ideas flowed into the 19th century, when the idea of genius became firmly associated with the exceptional individual who could create *ex nihilo*, out of nothing—whose work was wholly original. The artist became a kind of god.

This way of thinking was full of binaries. The distinction between genius and mere talent mapped onto that between art and entertainment. It also mapped onto the distinction between composers, seen as the epitome of creativity, and performers, who were merely recreative artists. And more than that, it mapped onto gender. Nowadays Clara Schumann is known as the wife of the composer Robert Schumann, but during their lifetimes it was Robert who was known as the husband of the most celebrated pianist of her time (Figure 11). Clara composed, too; as she wrote in her diary, 'I once believed that I had creative talent.' But she continued, 'I have given up this idea; a woman must not wish to compose—there never was one able to do it.' All this amounts to what—borrowing from the title of Beethoven's Third Symphony—can be called the heroic or 'Great Man' conception, according to which Great Men are the true agents of history.

In music the old idea of the artist as mediator of a higher state of being survived into the 20th century, as represented in Figure 12, which shows the composer Hans Pfitzner being inspired by celestial musicians. As I mentioned, the idea developed that great music—the music of the geniuses—was conceived in a flash of inspiration in which the whole composition was given to the artist at once: all that remained was to write it out. Mozart had said so in a frequently quoted letter:

> The whole, though it be long, stands almost complete and finished in my head, so that I can survey it in my mind like a fine picture or a

11. Adolph von Menzel, *Joseph Joachim and Clara Schumann*. Pastel drawing from 1854, now lost. Clara Schumann (1819–96) is shown accompanying the Hungarian violinist Joseph Joachim (1831–1907), perhaps the most highly regarded violinist of his day.

comely form at a glance...The committing to paper is done quickly enough, for everything is...already finished; and it rarely differs on paper from what it was in my imagination.

And Beethoven had confirmed it: the composition 'rises, grows upward, and I hear and see the picture as a whole take shape and stand forth before me in my mind as though cast in a single piece, so that all that is left is the work of writing it down'.

Of course, as I showed in Chapter 2, this account of Beethoven's compositional process is completely at odds with the evidence of Beethoven's sketches. The explanation is simple. The quote ascribed to Beethoven comes from the recollections of the pianist

12. Karl Bauer, painting of Hans Pfitzner (1869–1949), from the cover of the Munich-based magazine *Jugend* (1904). The figures in the background are a reference to Pfitzner's opera about the 16th-century Italian composer Giovanni Pierluigi da Palestrina, whose *Missa Papae Marcelli* was supposedly inspired by angels.

and composer Louis Schlösser: he said Beethoven had personally told him this in 1823—but it was not until 57 years later that he revealed it, and it is all too transparently modelled on the quote ascribed to Mozart. That in turn was concocted in 1815 by Johann Friedrich Rochlitz, who published it in the musical journal he edited, under the title 'A Letter by Mozart to the Baron von P'. Neither Mozart or Beethoven had ever said such things. They represent what 19th-century musicians and critics thought they ought to have said. They were part of the mythology around which the retrospective image of big-C Classical music was constructed. It is entertaining—or sad, depending on your point of view—to see later composers, such as Max Reger, making out that they composed in precisely that way, when the evidence of their sketches is that they did nothing of the sort.

A new conception of the musical work emerged in tandem with this idealization of the composer, and here there is some more historical background to put in place. Until around the turn of the 19th century it was taken for granted that music was like throwaway fashion: it had a short shelf life. There were a few works that defied the passage of time, such as Gregorio Allegri's *Miserere* and Handel's *Messiah*, but they were the exception. Even Bach's *St Matthew Passion*, first performed in 1727, had hardly been heard since the 1740s, and not at all outside the Leipzig church for which it was written. So when in 1829 the composer Felix Mendelssohn organized a performance of it at the Berlin Sing-Akademie, this expressed a quite new idea: great music is not just for its own time but for all time. And because musical works were seen as timeless, the idea developed of a gradually accumulating canon of permanent masterworks (that word again)—an idea better expressed by Figure 13 than by anything I can put into words.

There are two aspects of Cole's fantasy that are particularly relevant to music. First, it represents an act of gatekeeping, implicitly asserting that these are the world's greatest, most

13. Thomas Cole, *The Architect's Dream* (1840). An American (but English-born) painter, Cole executed this oil painting for the New Haven architect Ithiel Town. It is an assemblage of what Cole—who had himself dabbled in architecture—saw as the greatest historical styles: Egyptian, Greek, Roman, and Gothic. Each building looks as if newly completed.

timeless architectural styles. In the same way, the musical canon set the standards that the production of later times would have to meet if it too was to enter the canon (and critics and historians would act as gatekeepers). Second, as the embodiment of permanent values, musical works became monumentalized as fixed and unchanging entities, the sonic equivalent of the stone-built monuments to human achievement that sprouted across Europe's capital cities in the 19th century. And here we can make a link between aesthetic or philosophical thinking about music and the practice of its performance.

This is where I come back to topics, the system of musical representation through which Mozart's piano music became 'a miniature theater of human gestures and actions'. How would this music have been performed in Mozart's time? According to Allanbrook, performers would have sharply distinguished the various topics—with their evocation of different places, styles, or emotions—from one another: as she put it, they would have brought out the 'flashy collage of gestures'. As usual with performance there is little direct evidence for this, but there is one suggestive detail: the use of slurs, the curved lines in scores that link groups of notes together.

In their piano music 18th-century composers such as Mozart used many short slurs, implying a series of separate gestures. But in the 19th century, editors cleaned up and regularized their notations, putting these canonic works into what they saw as an authoritative, permanent form. This included replacing those many short slurs with a few long ones, often following the phrase structure. And among all of Mozart's sonatas the most famous example of this is the opening of the Sonata in F major, K 332 (the piece Allanbrook described as a 'miniature theater'). Nineteenth-century editions show a single, four-bar slur. This fits with the legato style of what in Chapter 1 I called the 20th-century performance mainstream: recording this movement on the modern instrument, pianists from Robert Casadesus (1940) to Alicia de Larrocha (1989) project these bars as a single continuous phrase, creating a sustained, singing sound throughout it. Everything is smoothed out. Rather than being strongly expressive, personal interpretations, these performances are serene, restrained, you might say classical.

But are they Classical? The fortepianists I also mentioned in Chapter 1, playing the much lighter piano of Mozart's time, have developed a quite different way of playing this sonata. They bring out Mozart's short, repeated slurs in the first four bars, fragmenting the mainstream performers' single sustained phrase into a series of separate gestures (one of these performers, Malcolm Bilson, calls them sighs). The Dutch fortepianist Bart van Oort's recording, from 2005, characterizes each of the topics in this movement quite differently—the repeated shifts from one character or register to another create Allanbrook's flashy collage of gestures—and more than that, his tempo is constantly changing. Instead of there being a steady beat that continues regardless of what is happening, it is as if every gesture shapes its own tempo. The performance brims with detail. I don't say this is how the music was played in Mozart's day, let alone by Mozart himself: that's far too big a claim to base on a few slurs. But if, having got used to the fortepianists' conception, you listen again to a mainstream recording of K 332, it sounds like Cole's painting looks: it is a monumentalized music, the sonic equivalent of architecture.

Nineteenth-century ideas of music emanating from some higher plane accessible only to the geniuses have not entirely dissipated. The idea of musical works as ideal, timeless entities received by their composers in a flash of inspiration is echoed by the contemporary composer Antony Pitts, when he writes of his choral piece 'Love bade me welcome' that 'from the moment I started working on it, it was clear in my mind that this piece existed—complete, perfect, and (to me at least) unutterably beautiful and heart-rending'. But it is in performance that the presence of the past has been most strongly felt. In Chapter 1 I mentioned the idea—highly influential throughout much of the 20th century, and by no means defunct in the 21st—that performers should not interpose between the composer's work and the audience, but should rather efface themselves: it was said that when the late 19th-century pianist and conductor Hans von Bülow played Beethoven you were not aware of Bülow, only of Beethoven, and this was intended as high praise. (It was also said that the first of the great piano virtuosi, Franz Liszt, played best when sight-reading, because after that he could never restrain himself from improving on what was in the score.)

Again like so many of the classical music myths inherited from the past, this kind of talk really did not—and does not—reflect reality. I spoke of classical music fans, and virtuosi like Liszt were feted in much the same way as pop stars: young women swooned before him just as their successors screamed at the Beatles. Besides, the vast majority of compositions were not intended as candidates for the canon. Many were designed as showcases for virtuosity, usually the composer's own. There was a time in the 1830s when piano technique was rapidly advancing and little else was to be heard, culminating in 1837 with a staged 'duel' between Liszt and his rival Sigismond Thalberg (a practice echoed in the jazz duels for which saxophonists Dexter Gordon and Wardell Gray, among others, were famous). The traditional histories of music I mentioned in Chapter 1, in which performers—and hence women—hardly appear, are sometimes selective almost to the point of qualifying as fake news. That is the gatekeeping I spoke of.

And it's in this light that you have to read such recent statements as 'the experience of listening to a live performance solicits attention more for the performers and the event and far less for the work than is perhaps generally admitted', or 'there is much less work being done by the score and much more by the performer than is implied by the way we habitually talk about scores'. What is striking is that academic writers about music—here Carolyn Abbate and Daniel Leech-Wilkinson—still need to say such apparently obvious things. And on top of this we have the unwelcome aspect of HIP's otherwise positive legacy: the assumption that in music, unlike in other performing arts, performance must necessarily aim at historical authenticity. As Leech-Wilkinson says, this taken-for-granted principle is enforced by further gatekeepers—conservatory examiners, competition judges, concert promoters, critics—and the effect is to stifle creativity and undermine students' readiness to make their own decisions.

And these unhelpful ways of thinking lie behind what is widely seen as the most pressing problem in classical music culture: the decline of its concert audiences. Twenty-five years ago the American musicologist Lawrence Kramer was already sounding the alarm. 'This music is in trouble', he said, 'its audience is

shrinking, graying, and overly pale-faced.' You can see why. If
performers were to efface themselves and let the music speak for
itself, that militated against basic ideas of engaging the audience,
projecting the music to them, entertaining them. The result was a
norm of drab presentation, stiff gestural presence on stage, and
colourless, over-formal clothing; for the influential classical critic
Alex Ross, 'the overarching problem of classical music is the
tuxedo'. On top of that was the unwelcoming, and for novice
listeners alienating, etiquette of classical concerts: for example it
was wrong to clap after individual movements of multi-movement
works, however enthusiastic you were—a prohibition taken to be
timeless but actually dating back to around 1900, and enforced by
humiliating glares from other audience members. Concerts
conveyed middle-class exclusivity, and the diminished social and
multimodal dimensions of live musical experience meant it offered
little more than you could get from a recording. Many classical
music lovers concluded it made more sense to stay at home.

As in Chapter 1 I have been putting all this in the past tense
because things have changed since Kramer wrote. HIP may have
left an unhelpful legacy of historicism but it certainly diversified
what you could hear on stage. Organizers of classical concerts
have opened up their programmes: in 2019 the Proms, the UK's
flagship concert series, included an evening of Duke Ellington's
sacred music, a Nina Simone tribute concert, and an orchestral
work by Radiohead's lead guitarist Jonny Greenwood. And there is
more attention to stage presence. A few performers, such as the
Chicago-based new music ensemble eighth blackbird,
choreograph their performances, using the whole stage as rock
and pop musicians do; it is increasingly common for classical
recitalists to address audiences with the same kind of relaxed,
personal introduction to the next piece you expect from jazz or
rock musicians. Strict dress codes have been relaxed, and in
general the atmosphere of classical concerts is less forbidding
than it was.

Yet it's a far cry from the social experiences of music in the New York of the early 1960s where Kramer learned to love classical music. 'Some of my most vivid memories of the time', he writes, 'involve summer nights in a stadium filled with people from all walks of life, from all over the city. The acoustics were terrible; the pleasure was overflowing; the ovations were long and noisy.' Of course the present is never as good as the past seen in retrospect. All the same, the social dimension of classical concert-going remains impoverished by comparison with other musical genres and traditions, and inherited ways of thinking about music contribute to this. It's not just the tuxedos.

Beyond authorship

If you stopped people at random in the streets of Vienna in 1800 and asked them to name the outstanding musicians of the previous quarter-century would they have said Haydn, Mozart, or Beethoven? A century later, did they know they were living through the highpoint of Viennese modernism (not just Gustav Mahler and Arnold Schoenberg but a galaxy of celebrated writers and painters)? Probably not. All history—not just fake news—is built on processes of selection that filter out the vast majority of what happened and retain just enough to construct an intelligible narrative that is then taken to stand for the whole. And as we approach our own time it becomes increasingly hard to tell a story: there are too many facts and you don't know which are the important ones. But I think there is more than that to the ubiquitous sense that today's musical culture has become drastically fragmented, that now there are no big, coherent stories to be told. Actually that is a big story in itself. But there is also another: a move away from basic aesthetic tenets that until recently conditioned the idea of music in the West, and towards a quite different conception of what I shall call music as lifestyle. I am beginning that story here, but it is closely tied up with digital technology and I will complete it in the next chapter.

At one level, the story of musical modernism—meaning the classical tradition as it took on principles of modernist aesthetics shared across the arts in the 20th century—is one of constant and dramatic change. In terms of composition there was the development of atonality (music without the traditional organization round a 'home' key), of serialism (music built on strict sequences of pitches), of experimentalism (getting away from tradition and bringing music back to first principles), of minimalism (based on repetitive, sometimes mesmerizing patterns and creating crossovers with the groove-based genres of popular music), and of any number of other isms. Then there are the many composers who continued working in established styles—what you might call classical MOR (middle of the road)—and rarely made it into the history books that focused on stylistic innovation. The history books also ignored the vast majority of what actually went on in the 20th-century culture of classical music, which was performing and listening to earlier music. In performance, as we've seen, there was significant change, while technology brought about drastic changes in listening practices too.

But despite all this innovation and diversity, the classical-modernist tradition generally remained committed to more or less the same underlying aesthetic principles, the same basic conception of what music was and who it was for. Even if classical fan culture had subsided from its post-Beethoven peak, the culture as a whole remained strongly oriented towards composers as authors: they were the focus of aesthetic interest. Innovation was still a condition of admission into the canon, and in post-war avant-garde circles (including the improvisation ensembles I mentioned in Chapter 1) it became an obsession. And values of authenticity remained strong. For many composers, being true to your artistic principles meant writing music that was accessible only to a relatively small, if enthusiastic, public; for some, that was the proof of their authenticity. Challenged over the inaccessibility of his music after his *Panic*—composed for the last night of the 1995 BBC

Proms—attracted more complaints than anything else in British television history, the veteran British composer Harrison Birtwistle replied testily, 'I don't think that creativity is negotiable. It's for those who appreciate it. I can't be responsible for the audience. I'm not running a restaurant.'

It would be easy to pin the blame for the loss of public interest that came with musical modernism (so different from what happened in the visual arts) on composers who set too much store on their own authenticity—on gaining entry into the canon—and too little on what listeners wanted. After all, the canonical composers of the 19th century took themselves very seriously and yet managed to incorporate whistleable tunes and foot-tapping rhythms into their music. But this narrative of blame isn't entirely convincing. For one thing, it was late in the day for Birtwistle to be saying what he did. In the final decades of the 20th century the old values of compositional authenticity began to crumble, giving way to a new eclecticism and pragmatism. Composers were increasingly ready to interact with other music—old music, popular music, world music, music for amateurs—and to work across the long-standing divisions between art and entertainment. In the years after 2000 new music came out of concert halls and was staged in pubs, clubs, or underground car parks. But these developments did little to change the pattern of small, committed audiences.

Then again, the declining public interest that came with 20th-century modernism is just part of the broader decline Kramer spoke of. And the principal factors behind that came not from within music but from changing technology, the rise of mass culture, increased international travel, and the sustained migration that resulted in the establishment of large diasporic communities. Also key was the development of youth culture after 1950, within which music—particularly rock 'n' roll and its innumerable successor genres—played a key role. Music was both a badge of identity and a means of exclusion: in those days most parents hated rock 'n' roll, and that was part of the point. The same continues to happen through the constant proliferation and morphing of popular music genres, so establishing rapidly changing subcultures. For diasporic communities, too, music serves as a badge of identity: bhangra, for example, has its origins in the North Indian state of Punjab, but developed rapidly into a hybrid British–Punjabi genre. Throughout the Western world these factors, with issues of identity at their heart, have resulted in an explosion of parallel musical worlds.

As compared to the 19th century—when 'music' as defined by the arbiters of culture meant little more than Bach to Brahms—it was inevitable that classical audiences would be squeezed. And as the post-1945 generation of rock and pop musicians aged, former rebels joined successful classical musicians as establishment figures. Dylan's foundational role in post-war popular music, for example, can be largely understood on the classical model. As with Beethoven, there is the personal commitment to and identification with the artist: the heckler at the Manchester concert was saying Dylan had betrayed that commitment. There is the same idea of inscription in the canon: the *New York Times* described the release of a thirty-six-CD set containing Dylan's complete live recordings from 1966 (including the Manchester concert) as 'a monumental addition to the corpus'. And the singer was inducted into the Rock and Roll Hall of Fame (Cleveland, Ohio) in 1988, while the award of the 2016 Nobel Prize for Literature extended his canonical status beyond music, prompting debate about the nature of canonicity.

In many ways the dynamic of popular music is different today, not least in the changed balance between the predominantly male pioneers of rock and the increased representation of women among top-ranking artists: think of Beyoncé, Rihanna, or Ariana Grande. Even when it seems things have not changed since the generation of pioneers, they often take on new meanings. Consider Beyoncé. She is not currently eligible for induction into the Rock and Roll Hall of Fame (you are not considered until twenty-five years after your first record release), but she is already being monumentalized: as early as 2014 she had her own dedicated exhibit there, and the curator explained, 'We felt that [Beyoncé] really needed to take her rightful place alongside Aretha Franklin and the Supremes and Janis Joplin.' And the same applies to authenticity. Beyoncé had her own Ashlee Simpson moment in 2013: she was accused of cheating because she had lip-synched 'The Star-Spangled Banner' at Barack Obama's second inauguration in 2013 (she explained she had not had time to set up properly). Now, however, controversies around authenticity seem to revolve less around music than around race. In 2008 there was controversy over the apparent whitening of Beyoncé's skin in press advertisements for cosmetics company L'Oréal. And more recently Grande—who is of American Italian descent—has been accused of darkening her skin and appropriating African American Vernacular English both on and off stage. At stake in these controversies are issues of cultural ownership, always a sensitive issue in the tangle of hybrid traditions that make up popular music.

But gender is no less fundamental to the new dynamic. I said that foundational figures of rock can be accommodated within a Beethovenian model of greatness, and the masculinism of 20th-century rock stars finds its contemporary equivalent in the sometimes overt misogyny of hip hop. I also linked Beethoven to the idea that history is created by Great Men, and Figure 14 vividly conveys the fetishization of masculinity that is inherent in that world view. This aggressive gendering of creativity renders it highly exclusionary, as reflected in Clara Schumann's belief that women should not even wish to compose. Equally it genders the sense of identification with the composer that was central to the classical star culture. But while ideas of identification and intimate access to the star remain deeply embedded in popular music today, they have now taken on a very different quality that owes much to celebrity culture. The sociologist Jo Littler describes celebrity as a

14. Kaspar Clemens Zumbusch, Beethoven monument in the Beethovenplatz, Vienna (1880). Set in a leafy square, this bronze figure sits on a lofty pedestal surrounded by classical statuary, towering above onlookers.

media construct that purports to provide 'privileged access to the alleged "real" person "behind" a distanced, glossy façade of superstardom'. As Littler's language and punctuation convey, identity itself becomes a media construct, something created through the manipulation of appearances and associations—as illustrated by Beyoncé's and Grande's manipulation of skin colour. And this focus on mobile identity and self-fashioning is one of the things that flows into the culture of music as lifestyle.

In contrast to the overt gendering of the Beethovenian model of creative exceptionality, the celebrity model is readily available to women, as also to people of colour. But the forms of identification and intimacy that it affords are of a frequently objectifying, sometimes prurient, and ultimately limiting kind (Figure 15). It perpetuates long-established tendencies to see women as industry puppets rather than as authorial agents in their own right. This is not to say that women cannot break out of these limits, but to do so they have to work consistently against the grain. Beyoncé in particular is exceptional for the tight authorial control she

15. Article from the online news website *Huffington Post*, 25 July 2019.

exercises, as illustrated by her *Lemonade* project (2016)—hailed by *Billboard* as 'a revolutionary work of black feminism'—of which she said her aim was 'to create a body of work that would give a voice to our pain, our struggles, our darkness and our history'. 'Our' refers to the lived experiences of Black American women, and Beyoncé referred again to race during her set at the 2018 Coachella Valley Music and Arts Festival: 'Coachella, thank you for allowing me to be the first Black woman to headline'. The report on Beyoncé's Coachella set in *Harper's Bazaar* reinforced celebrity stereotypes when it told its readers that 'every facet of Beyoncé's personality was explored, as her costumes ranged from casual sportswear, to flawless, regal robes'. The issues of identity Beyoncé explores, however, go a bit deeper than that.

In this way the old idea of intimate access to the star remains, but it is informed by a changed value system. This is what I meant when I spoke of the new dynamic of popular music, and it has as much to do with society and culture in general as with music. The historical role of classical music as the taken-for-granted high-cultural expression of Western civilization was built on a network of interlinked ideas that included masculinity, whiteness, greatness, national destiny, the colonial order, and a future understood as firmly grounded on the status quo. (These values, too, can be read into Zumbusch's Beethoven monument.) All of that is far removed from the world of fragmentation, cultural pluralism, and an uncertain future within which music operates today—a world in which all musics, even Beyoncé's, Rihanna's, and Grande's, occupy niches (some niches are bigger than others). Apologists for classical music tend to emphasize those rare occasions when classical artists acquire a mass audience and celebrity status, for example the success of the Three Tenors following their appearance at the FIFA World Cup in 1990. But seeking to legitimize classical music that way only perpetuates unrealizable expectations that the clock can be turned back. It makes more sense to accept classical music for what it is today, a niche in a musical world full of niches, and to celebrate both its impressively high standards in what it does and the enthusiasm it instils in its devotees. It may be a niche culture, but for all its problems it is a *successful* niche culture.

So far I have talked about just one aspect of the idea of music as lifestyle. But it has specifically musical origins too. The 19th-century musical tradition most directly linked to it is arguably opera. While opera continued within the Western classical tradition after 1900, many opera composers began to work in film music—particularly Jewish composers from German-speaking Europe who emigrated to the USA in the 1930s. That was just as the talkies—films that incorporated soundtracks—were beginning and Hollywood stood poised for world domination in the 20th century's most definitive art form. (Bollywood may come a close second, but then look at its name.) It is not just the pioneering role of people like Erich Wolfgang Korngold, who had been a successful opera composer in Vienna before emigrating in 1934. It is that Hollywood composers based their musical language on opera, in particular the Wagnerian music drama, in which music works not alone but as integrated with other media to create narrative.

In film, as well as in later multimedia genres such as television and videogames, authorship is inherently divided. That is, film and media composers work with screenwriters, film directors, and videogame developers, in some cases with creative ideas flowing freely between them. In such collaborative contexts traditional ideas of the composer's personal style, self-expression, or authenticity—of the composer as aesthetic focus—become increasingly peripheral. Even in the case of figures like Maurice Jarre, John Williams, or Hans Zimmer, you don't hear film music as the composer speaking to you: it is a dimension of a multimodal narrative. And it's not just film and media music, or the anonymous library music widely used in radio or television production, to which this applies. Recent developments in computer-generated music involving neural networks and artificial intelligence are rendering questions of authorship not just irrelevant but unanswerable. Given the extent to which the aesthetic categories of the classical tradition revolve around authorship and values based on authorship, I see this as the first of three linked and far-reaching thrusts away from classical assumptions about what music is and towards music as lifestyle.

The second of these thrusts is based on a related technology: sound recording, developed in the late 19th century but commercialized in the 20th. As with film, the 1920s saw an explosion that turned records into a mass mode of musical consumption; from then on, in simple statistical terms, recorded music *was* music for most people. A few conservative critics insisted that recordings were just an ersatz counterfeit of the real thing—live performance—and what is odd is that the music industry seemed to think the same way. Both their production techniques and their advertising focused on hi-fi (high-fidelity) reproduction, on bringing the concert experience as faithfully as possible into people's living rooms. Figure 16 makes the point, while a famous advertising strapline promised you 'the best seat in the concert hall'. All this built on long established thinking: just as performers reproduced the composer's work, so records reproduced performances. In fact, in the early days of recordings, listeners sometimes seemed to think of them as reproducing works and so bypassing performers. In either case fidelity was the watchword. The technology was seen in the traditional terms of authorship.

In the recording studios, however, something different was happening. Two technological innovations were critical: the development by 1950 of recording onto magnetic tape, which meant that recordings could be chopped up (literally, using razor blades) and spliced together in any sequence; and the take-up in the 1960s of multitrack recording, where up to thirty-two separate tracks could be recorded on a single tape, making it possible to build a recording track by track rather than recording everything

16. Advertisement for the Aeolian Vocalion gramophone, *c*.1914; compare the shadowy figures with the performing angels in Figure 12.

at once. (You listened to one track—e.g. a drum track—while laying down the next, and so on.) This made it possible not simply to reproduce the sound of live music, but to add something extra to it, to go beyond it. A simple example is the tightness and complexity of the studio recording of Queen's 'Bohemian Rhapsody', masterminded by Freddie Mercury (the other musicians laid down their tracks but had no idea what he had in mind); the band did play 'Bohemian Rhapsody' in concert—they were after all a rock band—but they had to simplify it and could never achieve the same precision.

There are more complex examples too. In opera there are the recordings of Wagner's *Ring* cycle made around 1960 by British producer John Culshaw. He used stereo to convey the positioning of the characters on stage, but he also had a bigger idea: rather than reproducing what you might hear in an opera house, he aimed to recreate by other means the emotions you might experience there. Another example is Glenn Gould, the first leading pianist to abandon the stage for the recording studio, who used different microphone set-ups and placement in the stereo field to express the music's structure, giving rise to a new kind of interpretation that combined performance and recording. Both Culshaw and Gould were using technology to create new, specifically gramophonic (in America phonographic) experiences. And both had prophetic ideas about how technology would in the future enable consumers to customize recorded music to their own preferences or mood—ideas that prefigured music as lifestyle but were realized only with the development of digital technology.

But the strongest connection between music and lifestyle was forged by radical changes in how, and where, people consumed music (and this is the third of my thrusts). In the 19th century, operas and symphonies were heard in the public spaces of opera houses and concert halls. In the 20th century both radio and gramophone brought music into homes. People listened to them socially, but later in the century high-quality consumer headphones also turned music into a solitary, immersive experience. At the same time transistor radios and later ghetto blasters brought musical consumption into the open air, while the invention in 1979 of the Sony Walkman—which played cassette tapes and came with earbuds—encouraged listening while walking, jogging, or cycling, in effect adding a soundtrack to people's everyday lives. And new ways of listening stimulated the development of new genres. Eno gave ambient music its name with his 1978 album *Ambient 1: Music for Airports*, while the hip hop genre G-funk was created by Dr Dre (Andre Young) specifically for in-car listening: 'when I do a mix', he said, 'the first thing I do is go down and see how it sounds in the car'.

In all these ways the separation between music and everyday life, maximized by the ritual of the concert hall, dissolved as music increasingly became a dimension of people's everyday personal environment. But these developments were just preludes to the transformations that resulted from digital technology, and so the story continues in Chapter 4.

Chapter 4
Music 2.0

Music, technology, lifestyle

The idea of music being natural has a long history, but we can start with the 18th-century political thinker, writer, and part-time composer Jean-Jacques Rousseau. By 'natural' he meant melodic, vocal in nature, and expressive, like contemporary Italian music—as opposed to what he saw as the excessive artifice and over-complication of French music. Rousseau's belief that music should be simple and heart-felt fed into emerging ideas of musical authenticity, as echoed over two centuries later by the broom-cupboard encounter between Piganini and Ry Cooder. The idea of the natural also lay behind the heckle at Bob Dylan's 1966 concert: Dylan had sold out by abandoning his acoustic—natural—guitar for the electric instrument.

In the case of instruments the role of technology is overt. The piano enables its player to do things impossible for the voice, from rapid and unsingable broken-chord figuration to playing multiple lines and so creating a complete ensemble under one player's control. But technology plays a covert role too. As I said in Chapter 2, the coupling of body and instrument extends the mind, makes it possible to think and hear through instruments, even if they are not physically there. The same applies to the technology of notation, at least if you are a classical musician. Even if you sing alone, it is still conditioning how you think as you form sounds in your vocal tract. Then again, consider the operatic voice, which is natural in terms of biology but highly artificial in terms of culture: a trained voice is one in which a lot of time and money has been invested. And we saw that when in the 20th century the crooners pioneered a more naturalistic manner of singing, it was the new technology of the microphone that made it possible. In this way artifice, technology, and culture are intertwined, and without culture there is no music, only sound. That is why I spoke of music as the artifice that passes itself off as nature.

Technology, in short, is an irreducible dimension of music, and digital technology is simply its most recent manifestation. But what is the connection between music and digital technology? The answer lies in how sound is represented. Physically, sound consists of continuous waves of pressure that strike the eardrum. As an example of analogue—pre-digital—recording technology, a vinyl LP represents sound in the form of the hills and valleys within its half-kilometre-long spiral groove. When it is played back, the record player's stylus moves up and down, and these continuous motions, transmitted through a loudspeaker, recreate the original pressure waves. Digital sound, by contrast, involves sampling the pressure waves many times a second (44,100 in the case of a CD), so that a digital sound file consists of a vast series of numbers corresponding to the intensity of each sample. This conversion of sound into numbers—and of numbers into sound when the file is played back—means that sound becomes just another form of data. Computers can manipulate and store it like any other data. And because digital sound files are simply a series of numbers, they can be copied any number of times without loss of quality—unlike analogue recordings, which are inevitably degraded every time they are copied. The whole of digital sound technology is built on these simple principles.

Digital audio hit the marketplace in 1982 with the first commercially released CDs and players, and the format was immediately attractive to consumers: CDs didn't easily scratch like LPs did, they didn't require the same cleaning rituals, it was much easier to find the track you wanted, and they didn't suffer from wow and flutter (variations in the speed of rotation that made held notes waver up and down). But behind the scenes the transformation of analogue audio into digital proceeded by stages over several years. DAT (digital audio tape) recorders still used tape, but stored digital sound files on it; only later was the tape replaced by hard discs or solid state storage. Digital multitrack recorders and mixing desks replaced analogue ones, modelled on their predecessors but offering new features. Increasingly music production was based on DAWs (digital audio workstations), that is to say high-end computers with dedicated music hardware and software—though even today plug-ins for recording software such as Digidesign's Pro Tools may emulate earlier, analogue devices (reverb and delay, distortion, vocoder, and so forth). Bit by bit (literally), the analogue past has been overwritten by the digital present.

I can now extend the narrative of multitrack recording I began in Chapter 3. A basic principle of multitrack recording is to record each track 'clean', close-miking the singer or instrument so as to eliminate reverberation and extraneous sound. These clean tracks can be processed individually, and digital technology massively expands the possibilities for sound manipulation. Perceived errors can be fixed through pitch correction or quantization (snapping notes to the beat or sub-beat), and lipsmacks or breath sounds removed. This erases the traces of the body and creates the sonic equivalent of the perfect, Photoshopped skins you see in digital fashion photography; producer Steve Savage compares it to 'the contemporary obsession with depilation, deodorants, and the like'. Sound can be sculpted through digital filtering, while reverberation and stereo positioning can make different musical elements stand out from one another with a vividness unachievable in concert, or create acoustic spaces that could not exist in the real world. This is the specifically gramophonic experience that Culshaw and Gould pioneered, now transformed through digital technology.

I have been talking about studio-processed pop. But the same digital approaches were taken up, though more discreetly, in recordings of classical music—even as the industry continued to promise you 'the best seat in the concert hall'. In a book published in 2007, musicologist Adam Krims observed how, in a recent recording of an organ concerto by Carl Philipp Emanuel Bach (third son of Johann Sebastian), 'close microphone placement, spacious stereo imaging, and highly resonant space' meant that 'the activity of each instrument jumps out in unprecedented detail'. In contrast, he said, the highly resonant space of Anonymous 4's recordings of medieval music made 'the voices seem to float ethereally, losing their traces of corporal production'. Instead of coming from a single source, as in live performance, the music seems to be coming from everywhere. It exists in virtual rather than real space.

Krims links all this to the architectural qualities, decor, and other dimensions of contemporary urban living. In this new world, he says (and the italics are his), it is 'the *function of classical recordings to characterize and design an interior space*'. He also puts it the other way round: 'interior design for urban living now extends to sonic design, cross-marketed with other commodities more readily identified as central to the "lifestyles"' (he is referring, for example, to the 'loft lifestyle' associated with New York's SoHo area). But in reality such recordings amounted to something more than the niche fashion as which Krims represented them, based on a handful of releases from around 2000. By then this approach was becoming increasingly mainstream in classical music. Still touted for the fidelity of its reproduction of live music, recording was going beyond realism. It was creating something more real than the real thing.

But it is in the domain of personal music consumption—the last of the three thrusts I spoke of in Chapter 3—that digital technology has had its most drastic transformative effects. The story can be told in product launches. The analogue Sony Walkman was reinvented in the digital domain as the Apple iPod, which went on sale in 2001 and gave its users mobile access to their personal libraries of mp3 files; the introduction of smartphones such as the iPhone (from 2007) gave you mobile access to the entire musical resources of the internet. And since then smartphone technology has given rise to new dimensions of personalized listening. One illustration is music delivered in the form of apps. An early example was Björk's *Biophilia* (2011), which offered additional materials and game-like ways of interacting with the music, while a classical equivalent is the Stephen Hough's app release of Liszt's B minor Sonata (2013). But music apps are not restricted to recordings. For example, the iOS app Augment allows you to tune your sonic environment to your lifestyle or mood, both literally (you can autotune people's voices to the music you are listening to) and figuratively, for example by filtering out harsh sounds. As the website says, it 'harmonizes your listening experience' and so 'helps you to be less distracted and stressed'.

And just as the convergence of mp3 player and smartphone technologies opened up new possibilities after 2007, so did the evolution from downloaded mp3s (where there was no physical object but you owned the data) to streaming. With streaming you don't own the music. Instead master tracks are held on cloud-based servers and streamed on demand to consumers across the web; it's the music equivalent of Netflix. In the rock critic Robert Christgau's words, 'streaming creates the illusion…that music is a utility you can turn on and off…It makes music seem disposable, impermanent.' (Nothing could be further removed from Figure 13.) Streaming services provide access to gigantic music libraries and discovery tools to help you find the music you want, together with playlists of music for specific contexts or purposes. But they also incorporate or work with recommendation systems designed to help you find the music you didn't know you wanted. These systems had been in development since the early 2000s (Pandora Music and Last.fm were among the first), but the major change in consumer habits came when they were combined with comprehensive streaming services such as the current market leader, Spotify.

Music recommendation is rather like giving everyone their own, personalized radio station (hence Last.fm's name and Spotify's Radio feature). It's a bit like traditional programme planning—that is where the idea of playlists comes from—but the target is no longer a concert audience or a radio public. It is you. Music recommendation systems model your individual tastes; some are based on analysis of patterns of listening (the 'Users like you liked items like this' approach), while others are based on coding musical content. Some services push the role of their human curators (who aim to lead you to your next life-changing discovery), others trade on the sophistication of their algorithms (created by programmers whose aim is to put the curators out of a job). Increasingly recommendation factors in the context of your listening, such as the time of day or where you are. The latest concept as I write is affective recommendation: in one version of this, a selfie is analysed to determine your mood, with music being chosen to resonate with or perhaps counter it.

And this illustrates an increasingly significant aspect of music as lifestyle: care of self. As long ago as 1948 the World Health Organization defined 'wellbeing' as a positive state rather than merely the absence of disease, while in recent decades a new field has developed around the keywords music, health, and well-being. Strongly linked to such bottom-up initiatives as community arts and the natural voice movement, music is valued for its capacity to bring people together, promote inclusion, foster a sense of identity, and help in the regulation of mood. In this way Augment's promise to help you avoid distraction and stress represents a new take on a familiar practice, as does a new feature that Spotify introduced in April 2020, during the early stages of the Covid-19 pandemic: Daily Wellness ('a mindful mix of music and podcasts, refreshed for you morning and night'). Similarly Spotify's innumerable sad playlists update the long-established use of music as a tool for emotional self-management. But digital technology adds a further dimension. By tracking each individual's listening history, streaming services make it possible to 'look back on my past weeks and see what I was listening to. I can even go back and look at blog posts or coding sessions and line up the sounds in my head.' The quote comes from a blog by Mark Koester, who describes himself as an 'obsessive self-tracker', and tracks his listening alongside his eating, exercise, and so forth. Music becomes a dimension of the quantified self.

Koester's blog is called 'Tracking the soundtrack of your life', and the phrase suggests you are starring in your own personal movie, using music to define who you are and who you want to be. (That takes us back to the Prudential commercial.) Seen in this light, music becomes just one of many modalities of consumerist identity construction, along with the car you drive, the home decor you choose, the clothes you wear, and the food you eat. This is taking us back to the ideas of mobile identity and self-fashioning that I spoke of in relation to celebrity culture in Chapter 3. You construct and communicate—you perform—your identity by selecting from the plethora of choices that define consumer culture; it's rather like social networking sites such as Facebook or Twitter, where the nature and number of your friends or followers define who you are. And actually the domains of music and social networking have become more or less inseparable. Facebook and Twitter play a significant role in the dissemination of music, and conversely many music-specific sites (including Last.fm and Spotify) incorporate social networking features.

In this way digital technology starts as an improved way to do existing things—as with digital multitrack recording—but turns into a way of doing new, paradigm-busting things. It improves things only to substitute new things for them. Like its use for self-care and other aspects of lifestyle management, music's role as a badge of identity can be traced back before digital technology (recall what I said about youth culture), but technology affords its transformation into something existentially different. Music as lifestyle is music that is conceived or consumed in terms of a value system constructed not—as in the classical tradition—around musicians' expressive needs but rather those of listeners and consumers. Like Hodge's constructivist view of art, it might be seen as a more democratic conception of culture. Yet the more elitist, author-based values of self-expression and authenticity I talked about in Chapter 3 have by no means completely disappeared from the world of music as lifestyle. Old values rarely do. Rather they accumulate, so contributing to today's niche-based culture in which multiple genres and traditions coexist, all with their own, sometimes incommensurable value systems.

If these values are incommensurable, that may be because they reflect—and contribute to—different senses of self. The idea of the genius or Great Man, as personified by Beethoven, was grounded in 'the Western conception of the person as a bounded, unique, more or less integrated motivational and cognitive universe'. This is how selfhood was seen during the 19th century: autonomous, consistent, beholden to nobody, true to oneself (and there we have the link with classical ideas of authenticity). The quote is from the American anthropologist Clifford Geertz, who describes this conception as 'a rather peculiar idea within the context of the world's cultures'. And certainly it does not fit well with contemporary ideas of selfhood as something we fashion or perform (including in the musical sense), something that mutates according to where we are and who we are with, something that exists in and through our relationships with others. The result is a fluid sense of self that forms part of what was once called the postmodern condition (a term no longer fashionable).

In this way, just as ideas of stable, integrated selfhood have given way to mobile and performative identities, so today's musical culture—in which musics from different times, places, social groups, or ethnicities exist side by side—lacks the sense of fixed identity it had when 'music' meant the notated music of a Western, white, mainly urban bourgeoisie. Traditions such as rural folk music (unless metropolitanized through notation and added piano accompaniment) and Celtic music—even the Celtic 'art' genres such as pibroch—fell outside that definition of 'music'. And so of course did musics from other parts of the world. All these were foreign, other—and their very alterity reinforced the sense of fixed cultural selfhood. The world has changed since then, and the story I have told is by no means just a musical one. In fact there could be hardly be a clearer demonstration of how music does not dwell in some inaccessible heaven of Platonic forms but is part and parcel of broader sociocultural change in the here and now.

Digital participation and musical style

Among the most spectacular aspects of digital technology is its ability to reconfigure time and space. Time is reshaped in the recent spate of holographic performances by deceased artists, for example Tupac Shakur (d. 1996) performing at the 2012 Coachella Festival (Figure 17), or Michael Jackson (d. 2009) at the 2014 Billboard Music Awards. Space is defied in telematic music, made together in more or less real time by performers around the world (more or less because you can never completely eliminate lag). An early example, from 1998, is Seiji Ozawa conducting Beethoven's 'Ode to Joy' at the opening of the Nagano Winter Olympics (Japan), with synchronized choruses in Berlin, Cape Town, Beijing, New York, and Sydney. A more recent one is Avatar Orchestra Metaverse, a group of musicians based in three continents whose backgrounds range across contemporary classical and popular genres: their telematic performances take place in sometimes fantastical venues within Second Life. That means their audiences, though sharing the same virtual space, may in real life be situated anywhere in the world.

17. Holographic performance by Tupac Shakur (right) at the 2012 Coachella Music Festival, with Snoop Dogg on the left.

But if there is a definitive icon of music in digital culture it is Hatsune Miku, the fantasy Japanese schoolgirl powered by Vocaloid voice synthesis technology. Her holographic concert tours extend across Asia, Europe, and North America (Figure 18), but she is most ubiquitous in the form of anime-style videos made by her fans: there are 170,000 on YouTube, while as I write 2,312,489 fans follow her on Facebook. Ever since she was released in 2007 she has been 16 years old, 158 cm tall, and weighing 42 kg. She comes out of the highly commercialized real-world culture of Japanese 'idols', closely controlled teenage performers whose manufactured cuteness verges on dehumanization. That is why one of her fans says it is in Miku, rather than the flesh-and-blood idols, that authenticity is to be found: 'This is real. This is the real freedom of expression. Look at the idols, look at the girl groups. All fake.' Such conflations of the real and the virtual—of nature and artifice—pervade music in digital culture.

The fan videos of Miku make her an example of the new forms of participation afforded by digital technology. Another

18. Hatsune Miku, in concert at Le Zénith, Paris, on 16 January 2020.

comes from Eric Whitacre, the American composer who combines digital savvy with a New Romantic aesthetic and is best known for his choral music. In 2009 he created a Virtual Choir, based on thousands of people across the world uploading videos of themselves singing his music (so reconfiguring both time and space), and the Choir's fourth project, 'Fly to Paradise', has a remix dimension. You download the tracks from the Virtual Choir website and make your own mix before uploading and sharing it. Here it is Culshaw's and Gould's futuristic ideas about listeners customizing recordings that are being realized through digital technology.

But remixing goes further. The 'Fly to Paradise' remix project is a classical-music equivalent of websites such as Mashstix and Indaba Music, through which you again work with individual tracks or stems (groups of tracks) so as to create your own mix. Just as with 'Fly to Paradise', you share it with others, and this sharing is key to understanding what is going on. Mashstix and

Indaba Music are not just technological resources: they are hubs for communities of like-minded individuals. Mostly amateur, their members offer mutual support by commenting on one another's work, and the social aspect of the participation is as important as the musical. That is the dimension of digital technology's impact on music on which I am focusing in this section, but I begin by considering musical participation more generally.

In many musical cultures there is no clear division between amateur and professional music-making. In Western culture, where there is, the vast majority of musicologists have concentrated on music made by professionals. Yet an enormous amount of non-professional music-making has always gone on; in simply statistical terms, the professional music-making represented in the history books probably amounts to little more than a rounding error. And as with remixing today, this music-making has been motivated by purposes that have as much to do with community as with aesthetics. Tellingly, it took an anthropologist to think of something as apparently obvious as systematically researching the world of amateur music-making in a British provincial town, Milton Keynes: Ruth Finnegan documented it across schools, churches, pubs, and clubs, and across genres from classical to jazz and rock, and from brass bands to folk and country music.

Let's just list a few examples of participatory music-making. There are high-profile youth orchestras, sometimes associated with projects of national reconciliation (such as the National Youth Orchestra of Iraq) or social inclusion (the Simón Bolívar Symphony Orchestra of Venezuela). There are community choirs with similar aims but at a grass-roots level. There are small-town indie bands that give teenagers experience of extracurricular collaboration—sometimes continuing into adult life to compensate for unfulfilling jobs. (Parents who ferry teenage children and their gear to and from gigs know that widely voiced concerns about the decline of participatory music-making are misplaced:

that may apply to classical music, but you have to look at music-making in the round.) Then there are the do-it-yourself traditions of British popular music, illustrated by skiffle bands in the 1950s and punk in the 1970s. Brass bands and massed choral singing still exist in the North of England, but their heyday was early in the 20th century, when they were a major element of civic social life.

But the most striking demonstration I know of the sheer quantity of participatory music-making comes from the *Hofmeister Monatsberichte*, a series of monthly sheet music catalogues issued by the Leipzig-based music publisher Friedrich Hofmeister that began in 1829 and continued into the 20th century. (I know about this because I ran a project turning them into an online database.) No less than 330,000 publications are listed, the vast majority by composers even musicologists haven't heard of, and for equally obscure instruments and ensembles: there is for example a category of music for combined harmonium, physharmonica, and harmony flute (all small free-reed organs, now defunct). These are the relics of amateur music-making, mainly taking place at home in those pre-television days. And they are almost completely ignored by music historians, for two reasons. First, this is not where you look for the canonic music that gets into the history books. Second, there are simply too many of them. Music historians are primarily interested in the individual qualities of a limited number of works in a few elite genres; they don't know what to do with repertories numbering in the hundreds of thousands.

I ran into exactly this problem with another project, originally based on Queen's 'Bohemian Rhapsody' video—a leading candidate for the title of first ever music video—plus a few television commercials derived from it and the alternative visualization in *Wayne's World*. There was a near ten-year hiatus in the middle of the project (the book my chapter was intended for was pulled), and by the time I got back to it YouTube had come into being. I didn't record how many hits I got when I first searched on 'Bohemian Rhapsody video', but I do know that a search on 'bohemian rhapsody' AND 'puppet' yielded 304 hits. And apart from the famous Muppets version and the 303 others, there are versions incorporating imagery from *Star Wars* and *Star Trek* or from vintage videogames such as *Mega Man* and *Final Fantasy*; a host of anime versions, for example based on the *Neon Genesis Evangelion* series; versions visualized using Lego (there is a whole YouTube channel featuring Lego versions of Queen videos); versions featuring *My Little Pony*, Mount Rushmore, and obsolete digital detritus; and much more. Some use one or another of Queen's recordings of 'Bohemian Rhapsody', others use one of the many covers of the song, or remake it (including the digital detritus version, which uses the sounds of floppy disc drives). In my chapter I provided an overview of the different versions, selected a few (on no particular criteria) and discussed them in more detail, and speculated on the cultural significance of what was going on. I didn't know what else to do.

What was actually going on was an unforeseen consequence of the internet, originally invented for purposes of military and academic communication. In the 1980s the internet only supported text, but even then virtual communities developed. The best documented is the WELL (Whole Earth 'Lectronic Link), based in the San Francisco Bay area; members pursued a range of common interests from chess and cookery to the Grateful Dead (many Deadheads joined). The early 1990s saw the development of the World Wide Web, whose familiar architecture of linked websites supported images and sounds; around 2000 this morphed into so-called Web 2.0, which enabled the user interaction fundamental to everything from Mashstix or Indaba Music to social networking and online shopping. There was a mushrooming of online affinity groups based round shared interests, and music was one of them. Mashstix and Indaba Music both go back to the 2000s and incorporate some of the community-building features of social networking sites. General-purpose sites like YouTube were also equipped with features (such as comments, channels, and messaging) that meant such communities could form under its umbrella.

Henry Jenkins was the first media scholar to seriously research the culture of digital participation, including for example fanfiction based on Harry Potter. Fans of J. K. Rowling's originals write their own stories based on Rowling's characters, post them to dedicated websites, read and comment on one another's stories, and so build a virtual community. (Writing in 2006, Jenkins said the largest of these sites contained 30,000 fan-generated stories; now two of them each have over 80,000.) Jenkins also worked on fan videos based on *Star Wars*, which use easily available and cheap (or pirated) video editing software for similar purposes. He hasn't worked specifically on music, but it is the same kind of digital participation that lies behind the innumerable videos of 'Bohemian Rhapsody'—and of any number of other highly successful songs—that you find on YouTube. Digital technology has made it easy to create such videos, disseminate them to like-minded viewers, and so build a community around them. Community members subscribe to one another's channels and comment on one another's videos.

For Jenkins, these digital cultures of participation are a contemporary recreation of the traditional folk cultures ousted by film, television, and other mass media—what are sometimes called cultures of vernacular creativity. At one point Jenkins says his own grandmother was 'a remix artist'—by which he means she made patchwork quilts, buying scraps of remaindered cloth from local mills and sewing them together. 'She would have learned these skills informally', he comments, 'observing the community of quilting women as they worked, gradually trying her own hands at the craft and learning through doing.' In other words—like learning music in the days before conservatories—it was a communal practice, and it is this dimension that Jenkins sees digital technology as recovering. It is telling that he makes his point by referencing a form of musical participation: remix originated in Jamaica around 1970 and spread through deejaying and the development of the digital sampler before becoming ubiquitous on the internet.

The ethnomusicologist Thomas Turino distinguishes between what he calls presentational music (made by musicians for an audience) and participatory music (made by musicians for themselves). The distinction is fuzzy, but Turino's point is that it has an impact on musical style. For example, he says, participatory music is in open form (it can go on as long as people want it to), it is full of repetition (people who don't know it can pick it up as they go along), and dramatic contrasts are avoided (they would require pre-planning and rehearsal). Presentational music has the opposite characteristics. In other words participation conditions musical style, and digital participation is no exception.

Consider that paradigmatic product of digital culture, the internet meme. Once again this is the digital continuation of a pre-digital practice (think 'Kilroy was here')—and once again the speed and reach of digital technology transforms it into something essentially new. For media theorist Limor Shifman the key characteristic of an internet meme is that it induces people to copy, transform, or parody it: if it doesn't spread—if it doesn't go viral—it isn't a meme. And there are certain features that help with this. One is simplicity: it shouldn't be too hard to work with. Another is repetitiveness, which elicits imitation and enhances memorability. Others include whimsicality (an invitation for people to fill the gaps) and playfulness, especially when based on incongruity. Shifman is primarily talking about text and image memes, but her principles apply to music too.

An example is *Nyan Cat* (Figure 19). Its 177,189,182 views reflect the incongruity of the pop-tart cat sailing through the skies for all eternity with the stars flashing by, leaving behind a rainbow trail, coupled to the hauntingly whimsical—and maddeningly repetitive—music. (The image of the cat was posted

19. Nyan Cat.

by American illustrator Chris Torres; the music was created for Hatsune Miku; and they were put together—arguably the core creative act—by the anonymous YouTube user saraj00n.) Or consider the Korean artist Psy's *Gangnam Style* (3,603,572,130 views), actually a full-length music video but one that spread like a meme: for Koreans it is a satire on crazy rich Asians, for the rest of the world it is whimsically inscrutable and full of incongruity, with its repetitiveness and idiosyncratically imitable dance adding to its 'spreadability'. Both, but especially *Gangnam Style*, have spawned innumerable recreations, usually with some kind of parodistic intent (*Mexi Style*, *Aussie Battler Style*, *Mitt Romney Style*, and so forth).

Incongruity, whimsicality, playfulness: these are basic characteristics of digital culture, as evident in the media aggregation and discussion website reddit as in internet memes, or in such other key digital genres as video mash-up. Mash-up is [11] about incongruity. Eclectic Method's mash-up of Beyoncé's lies' and Lynyrd Skynyrd's 'Sweet Home Alabama' juxtaposes 2000s commercialism with the authenticity of 1970s rock, a symbol of contemporary Black female empowerment with a white band from the American South whose stage sets frequently featured a giant Confederate flag. Again, musicologist John Richardson describes mash-ups of death metal and Britney Spears as revealing 'the artifice that has always existed in constructions of heavy metal rock and the brutal truths that lie under the sheen of girly pop'. Each song unsettles your experience of the other, forcing together connotations and emotions that we like to keep in separate compartments. Unanticipated meanings emerge as the songs grate against one another. All this adds up to a distinctive digital aesthetic that is shared across different platforms, genres, and media—something that the technology affords, but does not determine. Technology makes things possible, but it takes people to create culture.

Selling sounds

I mentioned the virtual diva Hatsune Miku, and she provides a good example of the new forms of business based on digital participation. As I said, she is powered by Vocaloid software, originally developed by Yamaha: basically you type in your music and lyrics, and Miku sings. She is just the most famous of several virtual characters marketed by the Japanese music and media firm Crypton Future Media, and she comes as a package consisting of the Vocaloid engine, dedicated Miku voicebanks, and a Creative Commons CC BY-NC licence. A freeware animation program called MikuMikuDance enables you to make the anime movies through which Miku is best known, and while Crypton owns the rights to images of her (which is why I couldn't use one for Figure 18), the CC BY-NC licence allows you to post your videos on websites such as YouTube; you are identified as the author, and the only restriction is you cannot commercialize them. In this way Crypton's business model is designed for digital participation. It is based on an understanding of the values and motivations of the worldwide Miku fan community.

Henry Jenkins sees such monetization of what in business-speak is called 'user generated content' as the core of Web 2.0 businesses (his term). YouTube and Second Life exemplify this: people go on YouTube to see the videos uploaded by users, and similarly Second Life residents create the virtual landscapes, houses, shops, and clothes—not to mention concerts of live-streamed music in virtual bars—that transform Second Life from a platform into a virtual world and so attract more residents. YouTube monetizes user-generated content through advertising, Second Life through sales of virtual land. But Jenkins observes that, in contrast to Japanese Web 2.0 businesses, many American corporations have been slow to exploit this business model. Instead of seeing fanfiction as a means of building a community of fans, he explains, the corporate rights holders of both Harry Potter and *Star Wars* used copyright law to close down fan activities. They did not appreciate the potential of digital participation for both customer loyalty and sales.

Businesses that do not understand their customers, Jenkins warns, risk losing control of their own markets. And that is what happened to the music business at the turn of the 21st century. Digital downloads meant consumers could access music immediately. But record companies did not sell music that way. So their customers searched the web and downloaded it for free. The record industry responded by suing its customers, and the end result was it lost control of the market. But as in the previous section, I need to go further back in time, because to understand the impact of digital technology on the music business, you need to know how it worked in the pre-digital age.

As so often the story goes back to Beethoven's lifetime, and was long ignored by musicologists because of the old belief that music transcended mundane concerns. The premiere of Beethoven's Ninth Symphony (7 May 1824) was a financial disaster, and Romain Rolland—whom I mentioned in Chapter 3—wrote that Beethoven 'found himself poor, ill, alone but a conqueror: conqueror of the mediocrity of mankind, conqueror of his destiny, conqueror of his suffering'. For Rolland poverty only underlined Beethoven's artistic authenticity: money did not matter. In reality, of course, it was a vital concern for classical musicians, and Beethoven's lifetime spanned the transition from a musical economy in which leading composers were supported by the aristocracy to one based mainly on selling works to publishers and income from concerts. The problem with the Ninth Symphony premiere was unseasonably good weather, meaning people were out of town.

There was a massive development of the music business in the first half of the 19th century. That included the creation of commercial concert halls housing both solo and orchestral performances (this is when the piano recital came into being); civic orchestras were established, creating regular employment. But in economic terms what counted for more was the growth in middle-class domestic music-making. This was like a three-legged stool: people bought pianos; they bought sheet music to play on them; and they hired teachers to show them how to do it, so providing many musicians with their principal source of income. At the same time there was a chronic over-supply of musicians and teachers that lasted into the 20th century, and many musicians struggled to make ends meet.

In the first decades of the 20th century the new technologies of recording and radio opened up new opportunities. But most important was the development of silent films—in reality not silent at all, because musicians provided live music ranging from a piano to an entire orchestra in the largest and plushest cinemas. For a few years musical employment prospects never looked so good. And then, in the wake of *The Jazz Singer* (1927), it all came crashing down. *The Jazz Singer* was the first talkie, and cinemas everywhere were rapidly equipped for sound reproduction. Musicians across the world were suddenly out of work. And the problem was structural, because all three legs of the music economy were chopped off at once: new listening habits prompted by records and radio meant fewer people were making their own music at home, so they didn't need pianos, or sheet music, or teachers. The music business continued, but its main activity rapidly morphed from publishing music to making and selling records.

From around 1930 to near the century's end the record industry was highly profitable, for a number of reasons. Making records involved a significant one-off investment, but after that they could be pressed at very low cost and in effectively unlimited numbers: the more records you sold the more profit you made *per record*. And the key to selling more records was creating more demand for them—which is exactly what the growth of 20th-century popular music did. In addition a series of technological advances encouraged consumers to repeatedly replace their music collections: first there were 78s (shellac discs named after their notional speed of rotation), then vinyl 33s (from about 1950), stereo LPs (offering two separate channels of sound and so creating a spatial dimension), and finally, in the 1980s, the new digital format of CDs. I say 'finally' because for most users CD sound was quite good enough. It persuaded consumers to rebuy their collections (again), while record companies monetized their back catalogues by re-releasing them on CD. There was a boom. It lasted over a decade, but it couldn't last for ever. Eventually people finished replacing their music libraries and the record companies had exhausted the most saleable items from their back catalogues. By the 1990s sales were tailing off, and the industry entered a period of retrenchment.

And at this point the digital technology that created the CD moves centre stage. The decline of the CD-induced boom coincided with rapid expansion of the internet, the replacement of slow dial-up access by broadband, the development of cost-effective, large-capacity data storage, and the creation of compressed file formats that were quite good enough for normal listening if not for audiophiles. All this meant music could be disseminated in the form of mp3s downloaded to consumers' computers or mp3 players for listening to any time, any place. The trouble was that, as I said, the music industry did not sell mp3s. So you had to create them by ripping your CDs, swap them with your friends, or get them off the internet. By the late 1990s peer-to-peer (P2P) file-sharing websites had evolved, the best known of which was Napster: registered users remotely copied sound files from other users' hard discs, and allowed others to copy their sound files. Napster took off and at one point had 80 million registered users.

As far as the law and the record industry were concerned, this was piracy, and industry bosses convinced themselves that it was the source of all their problems. Following litigation, Napster was closed down in 2001. The industry also sued individual downloaders. Famous examples from 2003 include a 12-year-old girl and a 66-year-old grandmother whose computer, it was discovered, was not in fact technologically capable of downloading mp3s. Four years later the Recording Industry Association of America won a case against a 30-year-old woman from Minnesota, who was ordered to pay $222,000 for downloading 24 songs ($9,250 per song). It was in this context that the academic lawyer and political activist Lawrence Lessig cuttingly observed that the combined effect of copyright law and music business practices had been to 'criminalize a generation of our kids'.

This is a classic example of what Jenkins called media companies' 'remarkable willingness to antagonize their customers by taking legal actions against them in the face of all economic rationality'. One way the record industry's behaviour was irrational is that, as surveys showed, customers who shared files actually bought more music legally. And in putting their energies into lobbying governments and litigating against their customers, the record companies did not ask themselves basic questions about what their customers wanted: music that could be downloaded and listened to any time, any place. Others, however, did, and Apple's answer was its iTunes store, which opened in 2003 and allowed users to buy music legally and download it direct to their computer or mp3 player. Ten years later iTunes had 575 million active user accounts. There was a market all right, but the music industry had lost control over it.

During the period of flux after 2000 there was a great deal of speculation, much of it utopian, about the effects of digital technology on the music industry. Individual musicians and bands saw an opportunity to free themselves from the record companies and their notoriously exploitative contracts. Many experimented with different strategies for cutting out the middleman and selling their music direct to listeners. Arctic Monkeys, a band from Sheffield, gave away their music, initially in the form of CD demos and later via their website; through this they gained notoriety and radio airplay, which they built on by signing to the Domino label in 2005. In contrast the well-established group Radiohead used the internet to disseminate their music independently of their previous label, EMI: they released their seventh album (*In Rainbows*) as a download available from their own website, allowing fans to pay what they wanted for it—with nothing as an option. That was in 2007, and the following year saw the establishment of Bandcamp, a music-sharing site with social networking features that enabled musicians to sell their music online. This time the musicians set the prices, but fans could pay more if they wished (and 40 per cent of them did).

While artists were concerned to find new ways of selling their music, listeners looked forward to a utopian age when all music would be free. There might still be a place for the music business—but rather than being based on the music itself, many thought, the money would be in services provided *around* it. In particular, they reasoned that the bottleneck would be finding what you wanted in the vast new wonderland of free music. During the 2000s the focus was on organizing the music on your mp3 player through playlists, whether created by you or by others;

celebrity playlists were all the rage, and people wondered whether George W. Bush's iPod playlist, leaked in 2005, had been cooked up by his media strategists. (It had.) Entrepreneurs and start-ups, however, were playing a longer game. They were hiring programmers and music students in order to develop the music recommendation systems I talked about earlier in this chapter—and as I said, it was the combination of these and streaming that transformed the market.

While there are many streaming services—including YouTube and Apple Music—the dominant example of a comprehensive music-streaming service as I write is Spotify, which has around 220 million users worldwide. As well as searching for individual songs or accessing playlists of music for particular purposes (Spotify is said to host nearly 2.5 million user-compiled playlists of music to have sex to), you can choose between a variety of recommendation systems. And then there are Spotify's social networking features, which include integration with Facebook and Twitter. That means Spotify is not only an environment for finding music and for listening to it, but also for sharing it with others. In short, it has positioned itself as the go-to music hub within the universe of social networking.

In some ways Spotify, along with all the other services that digital technology has opened up, is a hugely positive development for music lovers. It's a no-brainer: Spotify gives you free access to an almost limitless quantity of music across multiple genres, all available any time, any place, and with sophisticated tools to enable you to discover it. It's yours for free if you can put up with advertisements—and if not, you can take out a Premium subscription, which also provides an enhanced range of services. In some ways it really is the utopia that digital optimists were dreaming of in the early 2000s. But there are some other sides to the equation. For one thing, most musicians make very little money from streaming; the web is full of their complaints. And there is also a quite different kind of cost to set against these benefits.

Spotify's business model is based on income generated through Premium subscribers; the primary purpose of the free, ad-based service is to bring in users who will then choose to upgrade. Many Web 2.0 companies work this way, including YouTube and Second Life, though in neither case is it their principal revenue stream. Spotify's problem has been persuading enough people to take out Premium subscriptions. As I write, less than half its users have, and when Spotify was floated on the stock market in 2018, for $30 billion, it had still to turn a profit (just like Twitter when it floated five years earlier). In order to make good this shortfall, Spotify went down the same route as other social networking services: the sale of data for advertising purposes.

If you have read Spotify's Privacy Policy, you will know that it collects such personal data as what you listen to and when, the playlists you create, and your interactions with other users. It also says that it may share your data 'in a pseudonymised format' with Spotify's marketing partners and advertisers. And while there is nothing unique about this business model, music-streaming services can claim a unique selling point: that music provides intimate access to people's emotions, indeed to their deepest, most authentic selves. It has been said that Google knows you are pregnant before you do, but it is Spotify that knows the best music to have sex to—and when you are playing it. The emotional salience and time-sensitivity of music explains the pledge Spotify makes to its partners: it can reach its tens of millions of listeners 'when they're most engaged…from morning to night'.

In the last few years, then, both the technology for selling and disseminating music and the business model on which it is based have been transformed in a way nobody could have predicted—though over a quarter of a century ago the new media commentator Howard Rheingold wrote that new technology would enable businesses to target their advertising in new ways. With remarkable prescience, he added that this might result in 'the replacement of democracy with a global mercantile state that exerts control through the media-assisted manipulation of desire'. Nowadays music is in the front line of such manipulation of desire. Concerns about the surveillance society have grown exponentially, but to most people the Faustian bargain offered by Web 2.0 companies is just too tempting. And anyhow, who reads Spotify's Privacy Policy?

Chapter 5
Music in a global world

Music and globalization

In 1492 Christopher Columbus set out for India but instead
discovered America. In his wake trading links were created across
the globe and programmes of conversion to Christianity initiated:
the ultimate outcome was European colonization of most of the
world and a massive shift of resources. And as Europeans travelled
they took their music with them. It was indispensable for
purposes of conversion; the Portuguese converted some 100,000
Japanese between 1541 and 1577, when Father Organtino Gnecchi
wrote from Kyoto that 'if only we had more organs and other
musical instruments Japan would be converted to Christianity in
less than a year'. As colonists settled they created a home from
home, and music was part of that too. Calcutta—present-day
Kolkata—became de facto capital of British India in 1771, and
within twenty years Longman and Broderip (of Cheapside and
the Haymarket) had opened a music shop. The harpsichords and
fortepianos they imported were played by the memsahibs and
their daughters; gentlemen joined the Catch Club, whose
concerts were followed by dinners with catches and glees—the
popular songs of the day—being sung into the small hours. For
those with more classical tastes the Calcutta Band put on
concerts featuring music by such composers as Arcangelo Corelli,
Handel, and Haydn.

Those three names would be at the top of a list of 18th-century European music exported around the globe, and when Mozart ribbed his teacher Haydn about how few languages he knew, Haydn retorted 'my language is understood all over the world'. By the 19th century opera was becoming equally international, especially in the colonies (or former colonies) of southern European states. In Rio de Janeiro, for example, it was at the heart of fashionable society, and a newspaper article from 1827 muses on the contrast between this and a luridly depicted indigenous culture:

> While Rossini's music enchants a brilliant group of spectators at the Théâtre Impérial...some Indians...a few hundred leagues from the civilized capital of the empire, dismember the limbs of a lost traveller, to the discordant sound of a cow's horn that serves as a trumpet.

Another, equally bizarre juxtaposition comes from Gabon, in Western Africa, where nine years earlier, in 1818, the English naturalist (and pianist) Sarah Bowdich encountered an albino slave from the reportedly cannibalistic interior, who 'burst out with the whole force of his powerful voice in the notes of the Hallelujah of Handel' (that is, the 'Hallelujah Chorus' from *Messiah*). 'To meet with this chorus in the wilds of Africa, and from such a being, had an effect I can scarcely describe', Bowdich continues, 'and I was lost in astonishment at the coincidence.'

But there is more to music in a globalizing world than picturesque encounters or the recreation of home comforts. Underlying both the Rio reporter's and Bowdich's words we can detect a reassuring sense of the universality of European music. Built into the thought system of colonization and empire was a belief in the absolute superiority of European civilization, seen as legitimizing a centuries-long process of economic and human exploitation. Figure 13 expresses one aspect of this, arrogating to the West the right to set universal values of architectural greatness (ancient

Egypt qualifies, India and China do not). Another aspect is the inherent universality of Western art, now acting as an emblem of imperial hegemony. Music in particular was seen—and not just by Europeans—as based on scientific principles and having an emotional reach that other musics could not match. And as the artifice that presents itself as nature, it naturalized the status quo, projecting empire as just the way the world is. It is because of its apparent naturalness that music has often been spoken of as a universal language. But this is a problematic idea. It's true that all cultures have something at least partially corresponding to what we call 'music', but it doesn't necessarily follow that there are universal features shared by all musics. The very word 'universal' should put us on our guard: as the postcolonial scholar Homi Bhabha says, 'universalism...masks ethnocentric norms, values, and interests'.

While music contributed to the legitimizing of empire abroad, at home it served as a means of representing foreign cultures, portraying them as both different and inferior. Music provides a textbook example of what the postcolonial theorist Edward Said called Orientalism, the use of cultural representation as an instrument of colonial or imperial power. By the 19th century, a stereotyped lexicon of alterity had come into being that included twisting, melismatic melodic lines and non-standard scales often featuring augmented seconds: it faintly echoed some Middle Eastern musics but was used indiscriminately to signify people outside the West, lumping them together as simply different. And such symbolization of cultural or ethnic difference reached an extreme point in the first half of the 20th century with the Virginia-born composer John Powell, a card-carrying segregationist (in 1916 he founded a Society for the Preservation of Racial Integrity). On the one hand he composed a Symphony in A based on diatonic (white-note) folk tunes and embodying a vision of pure, Anglo-Saxon culture; on the other he wrote a *Rhapsodie nègre* that builds non-standard scales into a thoroughly chromatic style (adding all the black notes), and culminates in a cannibalistic rite. Deployed this way, music becomes a means of constructing 'us' through the opposition to a vilified 'them'; for musicians like Powell, musical hybridity—the mixing or fusion of different traditions—stood for miscegenation and racial mixture. This is just one example of how music can become entangled with pernicious cultural values and act as an engine of division, and I will come back to it.

So far I have shown how music can serve the ends of political and ideological hegemony. But it can equally serve to neutralize, resist, or interrogate power. Music creates contact zones: in the anti-Semitic Vienna of 1900, classical concerts enabled Jews and non-Jews to share the same space and for a few minutes forget about race. I mentioned Sterling Brown's invocation of jazz as a kind of contact zone, while musical genres from gospel and folk to free jazz focused support for the American civil rights movement of the 1950s–60s. In 1977 the Sex Pistols' 'God save the Queen' articulated a generation's contempt for the post-war British establishment. From 1987 to 1991 music orchestrated the 'Singing Revolution' in Latvia, Lithuania, and Estonia: huge crowds turned out to sing patriotic songs, and all three countries achieved independence from the collapsing Soviet Union. And in 2012 the part-Maori singer, guitarist, and producer Tiki Taane embarked on a joint project with the New Zealand Symphony Orchestra called 'With strings attached'; it was set up in such a way that Tiki was seen as inviting the orchestra members onto his own cultural terrain, so inverting the normal practice whereby official white groups invited Black artists onto their terrain in an often empty gesture of inclusion. In the words of Oli Wilson, 'Tiki asserts authorship over the colonial experience, and defines the nature of this experience on his own terms.' And this illustrates a point I made in Chapter 1: rather than simply reflecting social or political ideologies, music affords agency—hence Wilson's reference to authorship—and in this way can throw light on undocumented aspects of subaltern experience. It adds light and shade to otherwise black-and-white colonial histories.

Like other arts, music has served as a means of asserting identity in contexts of decolonization and nation building. For a moment I move outside music to make the point. Brasilia was founded in 1960 as the new capital of Brazil, and designed as a uniquely thoroughgoing example of architectural modernism—a style that first developed in Europe before spreading across the developed world. Masterminded by the Brazilian architect Oscar Niemeyer, Brasilia is not a homage to Europe. It is rather a claim that international-style architecture is what its name suggests: a heritage that transcends the national or the regional. Brasilia is a statement that modernity belongs not to Europe or North America, but to the world. Yet this is not a distinction that you can read directly from the buildings. It is a matter of context and interpretation.

All this applies just as much to music. Western musical styles were introduced to Japan in the late 19th century as part of a comprehensive programme of modernization provoked by the encounter with Western economic and military strength. This did not just mean bringing in European musicians. The school system was reformed to include group singing in Western style and the teaching of staff notation, while Japanese musicians were sent abroad to train. China embarked on a similar process of musical modernization early in the 20th century, again as part of a larger cultural, scientific, and political programme. And in Shanghai this dovetailed with the development of Western orchestral music to serve the large expatriate community; the Shanghai Municipal Orchestra fulfilled the same role as the Calcutta Band more than a century earlier, but by the late 1920s it had acquired a regular Chinese audience. The focus on Western music was strengthened when in 1927 the Nationalist government funded the establishment of a National Conservatory (now Shanghai Conservatory). The foundations had been laid for the position Western classical music occupies today as the expression of a distinctively Chinese modernity.

20. Chinese orchestra. Featuring members of the BC Chinese Orchestra and Edmonton Chinese Philharmonic Association, this is from a concert entitled 'Enchanting rhythms of Chinese music' which took place in Edmonton, Canada, in August 2015.

As important as the introduction of Western styles was the modernization of traditional Chinese music, particularly after the Communist victory in 1949. New conservatories were created that embraced both Western and Chinese music; traditional instruments were modernized on scientific principles—for example through standardizing tuning and building them in different sizes to create families of instruments on the model of the Western violin family. As in other countries, large ensembles were created, modelled on the Western orchestra but using the newly modernized Chinese instruments (Figure 20). Folk music was also modernized, and official troupes formed that brought together the different, and originally unrelated, music and dance traditions that fell within modern administrative areas: music became part of the operation of the state. Modernization also included social practices. Traditional music was relocated from streets and tea houses to formal concert halls, and performed by state-employed professionals before seated audiences. It is these modernized musics that are now designated as 'traditional', while such genuine folk traditions as survive are likely to be denigrated as old-fashioned and amateurish.

But perhaps the most profound transformation resulted from the introduction of Western notation. In some countries modernization has involved the adoption of a new script; Turkey exchanged Arabic script for the Roman alphabet in the 1920s as part of Kemal Atatürk's programme of secularization and Westernization. But adopting a new musical notation is more drastic, because different notations may chop up musical sound in quite different ways. Western staff notation is based on seven-note scales with five chromatic notes, adding up to twelve notes in the octave. Musics outside the West often use very different scales, with more (or fewer) notes and splitting up the octave into different intervals. Again, staff notation assumes that there is a regular metre (strong beats fall at equal intervals) and that note durations are arranged in powers of two (half note, quarter note, eighth note, and so on); there are ways of representing different divisions—such as triplets, meaning three notes in the space of two—but they are clumsy and limited. Transcribing music that does not work this way into staff notation means shoehorning it into the categories of Western music, and so imposing a false sameness on it. It echoes the problems Sapir and Whorf encountered in translating native American languages.

The adoption of Western staff notation for traditional music at the new Chinese conservatories affected how the music was thought about and how it was played. In particular it militated against traditional practices of improvisation. Rather than memorizing individual notes, traditional performers on the *erhu* (Chinese fiddle) internalized the melodic and formal outlines of the pieces they played, together with the principles of how to elaborate these outlines in performance. Musicians might play the same piece quite differently on different occasions, or as compared to other musicians. In the post-1949 conservatories, by contrast, it would be carefully notated, rehearsed, and performed, much like a Mozart violin sonata. It became fixed. As far as the conservatory musicians were concerned, they were playing the same music as before, and their conscientiously rehearsed performances of transcribed scores meant they were playing it better—more scientifically, more artistically, more authentically. Western commentators saw it as a loss of tradition.

So far I have talked about the spread of Western musical styles, technologies, and ways of thinking across a globalizing world. But it goes both ways. Just as Europe appropriated the rest of the world's material resources, so it appropriated its music. The dynamic, however, is different. The British empire is generally represented in terms of white colonists confident of their own superiority and looking down on the natives. But read some of the literature from the last years of the empire, such as Somerset Maugham's short stories, and you will become aware of an under-narrated aspect of the imperial experience: the sense that subject peoples retained qualities with which Western civilization had lost touch. On the one hand there is the Eastern spirituality consciously echoed in the music of Gustav Holst and later feeding into the Beatles and psychedelic rock; on the other, a rhythmic, embodied vitality particularly associated with African and South American musics. And this is not just a European phenomenon. Western envy of the authenticity and prowess of Black minorities—not necessarily incompatible with a belief in their racial inferiority—is replicated, for example, in the attitude of Han Chinese towards China's ethnic minorities.

We can trace two-way flows in both literate and oral traditions of music. Within notated traditions I have spoken of the appropriation of Western music as an instrument of nation-building, mirrored in Western musicians turning to other cultures in search of musical renewal. But it gets more complicated. If learning about other traditions enabled Western musicians to see their own culture in new ways, the same is true of musicians outside the

West who discovered their own national traditions through their reflection in Western music (the classic example is Toru Takemitsu, who said it was through the American composer John Cage that he came to value traditional Japanese music). At the same time, the meaning of 'Western' blurs as musicians from China, for example, emigrate and become established in the West (I am thinking of composers such as Tan Dun or Qu Xiaosong), or when—much less commonly—composers from the West work in cultures outside the West to the extent of becoming recognized as insiders: a contemporary example is the American composer Marty Regan, seen in Japan as a leader in the creation of new music for traditional Japanese instruments. Music may be an engine of division, yet it can also dissolve barriers of geography, nationality, and ethnicity.

Meanwhile there has been an extraordinary degree of globalization in the primarily oral genres of popular music. Behind them is a long history of hybridity that began with slaves from many, culturally distinct parts of Africa being transported to the American plantations: there a new culture came into being that combined different African and Western traditions. Both in the Deep South and in the northern cities to which many African Americans later migrated, genres came into being that were characterized by rhythmic repetition, groove-based textures, distinctive forms of vocalization, and improvisation, with jazz in particular fostering developments in harmonic thinking without precedent in the classical tradition. This amounted to a new musical culture located within the West but largely based on different principles and practices; it is a major dimension of how 'music' came to mean much more than Western classical music.

This deeply hybridized tradition of American popular music spread across the globe, but it was not a simple trajectory from centre to periphery. Britain was an early adopter of American rock 'n' roll, but transformed it and exported it back to America (the 'British invasion' of the mid-1960s). More complex interactions developed when African American genres were taken up in Africa and re-exported elsewhere. And increasingly, global popular music was not just consumed but created across the world, with Cantopop, J-pop, and K-pop, for example, attracting global audiences. What—going back to its origins—one might call the Africanization of world music illustrates how ubiquitous cultural practices are products of complex transnational exchange. It also illustrates how cultural, economic, and political clout do not always operate in tandem.

Music is a global phenomenon because it is inherently viral. People can't help imitating what they hear, and so—like internet memes—music spreads between cultures at speeds limited only by transport and communications technology (from the 30 miles per day of horseback or 120 of a sailing ship to the 100 Mbps of a fast internet connection). The British rock singing style epitomized by Joe Cocker or Amy Winehouse is an imitation of white American rock singing style, itself an imitation of African American singing style. Descended from the tradition of blackface minstrelsy, arguably the foundation of American popular music, this musical blackvoice is not only a mode of vocalization and a nexus of cultural associations but also a form of ethnic role-play. It may seem astonishing that the *Black and White Minstrel Show* aired on British television as recently as 1978, but musicians are still blacking up vocally (and perhaps literally in the case of Ariana). And imitation gives rise to hybridization. A dirty word for John Powell, musical hybridity had come by the end of the 20th century to be celebrated as an expression of the creative vitality that results from the mutually respectful interaction of diverse musical cultures.

A decade or two ago I would have written that last sentence without a second thought, but now it sounds distressingly old-fashioned. In many parts of the world ideals of the productive coexistence of different cultural and ethnic groups have gone sour with the spread of neo-nationalism. And music is implicated in that too. The stereotyped language of 19th-century alterity that defined 'us' against an undifferentiated 'them' has its more recent equivalents. If in the 20th century white American singers imitated African American singers, there is a sense in which African American singers did so too: to be commercially successful they had to sing black—that is, sing the way American whites thought authentic Black singers should sing. Again this is mirrored in today's China: successful minority musicians have to conform to the expectations of the Han Chinese. In short, music remains racially stereotyped. And Powell's white supremacist compositions find successors in the alt-right and White power music found across most mainstream genres of popular music, as well as specifically neo-Nazi genres such as National Socialist black metal. Music can dissolve barriers of nationality and ethnicity, but it still acts as an engine of division.

One would like to think there is something inherently progressive about music, with its stylistic fluidity—its ability to adapt and assimilate—militating against the fossilized categories and invented pasts on which populism is based. But that is wishful thinking. Music may be a force for good or for evil. But it is just the force. People are responsible for the good or evil.

World musics

There is a sense in which the internet has turned all music into world music: you can hear just about anything from anywhere in the world—as long as you have a connection (for some people still a big if). It has created a global jukebox, an inventory of sounds accessible across the world. And offline many musical traditions have a global reach through diasporic communities and migrant workers, or through the involvement of musicians and listeners irrespective of geographical origin or ethnic self-identification. On this criterion Western classical music, jazz, and rock are all world musics, as are such traditions originating outside the West as Islamic devotional music, Bollywood songs, and the various forms of East Asian pop. There are also some particularly globalized genres within these categories: only a handful of countries outside central Africa do *not* have heavy metal bands, for example, and 2018 saw a 154 per cent increase in metal downloads across the world, the most in any genre (J-pop came next). And with its low cost of production—all you need is a smartphone—hip hop is everywhere. But in this section I am concerned less with the fact of globally distributed practices of production and consumption than with the idea of 'world music'. So I start with three uses of the term—one highly commercial, the other two more speculative— and then propose a fourth.

The first is what people think of when you say 'world music', and it has a precise time and place of origin. The date was 29 June 1987 and the place was an upstairs room in a North London pub called The Empress of Russia. Representatives of a number of London-based record companies met to discuss how they could more effectively market a developing genre that lacked a name but combined Western pop style with sounds from outside the West, both instrumental and vocal. The international success of Paul Simon's *Graceland*, released the previous year and created in collaboration with South African musicians such as the male choral group Ladysmith Black Mambazo, had demonstrated the potential of such a combination, but record stores did not know what bin to put it in and shoppers did not know where to look for it. Delegates at the meeting voted to call the new genre 'World music' (runners-up included World beat, which would have been more accurate, as well as Tropical and Hot beat). And at a follow-up meeting they agreed to spend £3,500 on a publicity campaign, one of the most cost-effective investments ever.

What delegates couldn't agree on was what World music actually was; all they could say is what it wasn't (reggae, jazz, blues, folk). As it developed under the World music banner, the genre might be described in the same terms musicologist/ethnomusicologist Kofi Agawu uses to describe the impact of Western music in Africa: it 'colonized significant portions of the African landscape', he writes, 'taking over its body and leaving an African dress, transforming the musical background while allowing a few salient foreground features to indicate an African presence'. In the same way, the pop style that had developed in the West but now pervaded the world provided the body of World music—its harmonic, rhythmic, and textural infrastructure—while local musics from outside the West added the dress: new instrumental sounds, playing techniques, or patterns of vocalization. The pop body ensured ready accessibility across world markets, the local dress provided novelty and a touch of the exotic. In effect musics from outside the West—'non-Western' musics—were lumped together as an undifferentiated other and reduced to local colour. There was a distinct whiff of colonialism by other means. But as a commercial venture the World music formula could not be faulted.

My next two examples of 'world music' were both put forward by composers and are in a sense mirror images. The first goes under the name *Weltmusik*, which is simply German for 'world music', and it is an idea that circulated widely in European avant-garde circles during the 1970s. The leading German composer of the time, Karlheinz Stockhausen, related it to his 1966 composition *Telemusik*—a tape piece he wrote in Tokyo that incorporates many musical materials from outside the West. In this piece, Stockhausen declared, his aim was 'not to write "my" music, but the music of the whole earth, of all countries and races'; three years later he claimed that *Telemusik* 'achieves a higher unity, a universality of past, present and future'. And four years after that he published an article entitled *Weltmusik* which envisaged the dissolution of the world's existing musical cultures and their reassembly into the utopian vision of a 'unified *world culture*'.

Stockhausen presents this as a collective project located on a level playing field, as when he says 'a European can experience Balinese music, a Japanese music from Mozambique, and a Mexican music from India'. But his words betray him. He speaks of how 'people from other musical cultures' must be fascinated by the perfection of 'the varnished black Steinway piano' (I have a lurid vision of savages from the dark continent bowing down before this new fetish), and a paragraph later he writes 'we must get used to the idea that European cultural standards will retain, and even intensify, their fascination for all other people'. In short his *Weltmusik* turns out to be a Eurocentric project after all, less a utopia than a fantasy of world domination in the tradition of Schoenberg, who fifty years earlier had claimed his invention of serialism would 'ensure the supremacy of German music for the next hundred years'. And actually, Stockhausen's talk of universality might have led us to suspect as much all along (remember Bhabha).

The mirror image comes from Chou Wen-Chung (Zhou Wenjong), a composer who was born in China but moved at the age of 23 to the United States and spent most of his career at Columbia University, New York. Chou's vision begins in a mythical past: the traditions of Eastern and Western music share a common origin, he says, and that is why we can still hear commonalities between them. But as East and West have diverged, each has lost touch with part of this heritage. Eastern traditions have retained key aesthetic principles that range from timbral sensitivity and spiritual cultivation (remember Holst and the Beatles) to the capacity to productively assimilate foreign influences; Western music has lost these but is superior to Asian music in technical terms (thematic development, counterpoint, harmony, tonality). In his own compositions Chou aimed at a 're-merger' that would combine the strengths of both. But he had a bigger claim: we are witnessing 'the confluence of all musical cultures towards a new mainstream of musical tradition', he wrote, an 'irresistible rush of musical tributaries towards a world music that we can witness in our own lifetime'. Chou died in 2019 at the age of 96.

All of these three visions of world music turn on the idea of a fusion or synthesis of Western and non-Western music

(Stockhausen's 'unified *world culture*'). Rather than stylistic synthesis, however, world music might be conceived as a global network of linked music-making that fosters interaction between cultures that are distinct but interconnected. Seen this way the (originally) Western classical-modernist tradition becomes a prime candidate, and indeed both Stockhausen's and Chou's visions of world music came out of it. When I described them as mirror images, however, I was overlooking a crucial difference between them.

Stockhausen's musical training was entirely Western. Chou, in contrast, had acquired experience in both Chinese and Western music before emigrating, following which he studied with the German-American composer Otto Luening and the French-American composer and pioneer of electronic music, Edgard Varèse. While committed to introducing an Asian sensibility into his compositions, Chou was a composer in the Western classical-modernist tradition, like Tan Dun (who studied with Chou at Columbia) or Qu Xiaosong (who also spent time at Columbia but later returned to China). A consequence of the processes of modernization that took place in so many countries during the 20th century is that classical-modernist composers—composers who work with staff notation or electroacoustic media—are to be found in almost as many countries as metal bands. The more successful ones travel internationally and sometimes pursue simultaneous careers on different continents. They may live in New York, London, or Shanghai, but they do so with knowledge of and a sense of relationship to what happens elsewhere in the world. They see themselves as an international community of composers located within different cultures but with a linked heritage. That is one sense in which classical music is a world music.

But it's not just composition. It's also the performance of existing music—the bulk of classical music-making and consumption the world over. That too is a world music, and not simply in terms of

the globetrotting of high-profile conductors and pianists. I spoke
of the early development of Western classical music in China as
part of that country's programme of modernization; it remained a
permanent fixture in Chinese public life—apart from a period
during the Cultural Revolution when political circumstances
drove it into private homes—and after Mao Zedong's death in
1976 it became a prominent expression of the new, internationalist,
Sino-capitalist China. In urban centres swollen by migration from
the countryside, 18th- and 19th-century European music became
part of an increasingly affluent middle-class society—much as had
happened in 19th-century Europe—and by the time of the 2008
Beijing Olympics classical music was a focus of national pride.
The National Centre for Performing Arts (Figure 21), a spectacular
titanium and glass structure approached by a walkway under its
surrounding lake and seating a total of 5,452, is located close to
Tiananmen Square and was completed in time for the Olympics.
It has its own resident orchestra, with a programme of
international tours. Meanwhile jet-setting virtuosi such as the
pianists Lang Lang, Yundi (Li), and Yuja Wang are seen as
cultural ambassadors for China.

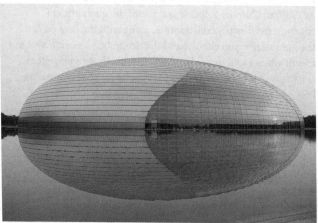

21. National Centre for Performing Arts, Beijing.

If that is another sense in which classical music is a world
music, then it is music in a world that is not just increasingly
globalized—economically and environmentally interdependent—but
also cosmopolitan, meaning that musics originally associated
with specific places, ethnicities, and histories have become links
in what might be called a culture of global connectivity. People
sometimes express surprise that Chinese musicians play Mozart so
well, as if the ability to play Mozart was somehow encoded in one's
genes. But we don't think about food that way. Nobody is
surprised if a French chef cooks Chinese food, and in fact it has
become something of a professional expectation that chefs master
a range of cuisines. The same is true of music: as the musicologist
Derek Scott says, 'professional musicians now find themselves
interpreting and performing music from a large number of
different cultural traditions'. And what applies to chefs and
performers also applies to their clienteles. We don't think it odd if
French people eat Chinese food or vice versa. In the same way
people decide whether they are in the mood for French classical
music, American 1970s rock, or J-pop—choices made possible by
their permanent availability on streaming services. They also
embrace more lasting affiliations to one style of music or another:
as I said in Chapter 4, this is just one of the modalities of
consumerist identity construction, along with the car you drive,
the home decor you choose, and the clothes you wear. It is what I
meant when I said music has come to embody a value system
constructed around listeners and consumers. This is music as
lifestyle, now in a world context.

There are those who think this kind of consumerist
cosmopolitanism—and the celebrity culture that is linked to
it—is as ethically bankrupt as it is ecologically unsustainable,
part of a global system built on social and economic inequity.
Ross Daly—with his Irish ancestry, English birth, and
specialism in the Cretan *lyra* the very model of a world
musician—makes a more focused attack on musical
cosmopolitans, sending up the

world music freaks kitted out with all the latest hi-fi gadgetry, surrounded by hundreds of CDs, records, and DAT recordings, who listen to West African griots one minute, Japanese Koto music the next and then Bengali music—and when you talk to them about the music, you realise they don't understand the first thing about the music, that they haven't got a clue about the cultural and human background.

His prescription? Forget records and instead listen to a great deal more live music. And Daly adds that until we do that—until we put the people back into the music—it is 'far too early…to talk about *world music*'.

Last words

Daly wrote that in 1992 (hence his reference to the now obsolete DAT format), but even then his vision of world music—the mutual, face-to-face encounter of musicians and music lovers from diverse cultures—conveyed a nostalgia for the old days when music was heard only at the time and place of its making. In reality music is much more frequently heard through earbuds or in complexly mediated forms such as the Prudential commercial with which I began this book, and it retains the potential to be humanly meaningful under all these conditions. And actually, the Prudential commercial exemplifies many of the dimensions of music's meaning I have been talking about in the course of this book. Just to cite a few, it depends on music's ability to connote deeply held values, and to communicate them almost instantaneously. It shows how music is wrapped up with people's identity and sense of self, while the voiceover speaks to viewers with the same quality of confidentiality—of vicarious intimacy and unmediated access—experienced by fans of Beethoven in the 19th century, Sinatra in the 20th, and Rihanna in the 21st. It is also the ultimate hidden persuader, as shown by the purely musical logic that positions Prudential as the solution to all your pension problems.

And it does this without your being aware of it. As the artifice that presents itself as nature, music slips under the radar. It has the power over people against which so many stories warn: the Sirens, whose enchanting song lured lovesick mariners onto the rocks; the Pied Piper, whose music persuaded the children of Hamelin to follow him into a cave from which they never returned; or the voice of Saruman in *The Lord of the Rings*, 'low and melodious, its very sound an enchantment'—the very model of the populist politicians who are wreaking havoc across today's world. Music, in reality a practice that is constantly changing, presents itself as not only natural but also immutable (remember how people resisted the evidence of early recordings). *Gagaku*, the long but discontinuous tradition of Japanese court music, was reinvented in the late 19th century and instantly became the audible symbol of Japan's ancient and unbroken nationhood. Western music introduced to Europe's colonies legitimized imperial power by giving it the appearance of universality. Music also naturalizes hierarchies of gender and race, so abetting the essentialization that reduces people to tokens. Race is not a biological given— there is a continuum of physical features and skin colours that belies cultural constructions of race—but music perpetuates such divisions through social practice, even as it has the potential to erase them.

Music, in short, can serve as an instrument of ideology, communicating values, hierarchies, and political beliefs while disguising its operation. Rooting out ideology is the business of critical theory, the aim of which the sociologist Max Horkheimer defined as 'to liberate human beings from the circumstances that enslave them'. And through Theodor Adorno (both a sociologist colleague of Horkheimer's and a composer who studied with Schoenberg's pupil Alban Berg), ideas from critical theory entered musicology in the 1980s and 1990s. It acquired a political edge that music history had previously lacked (at least outside Communist countries); traditional humanities-based approaches were increasingly supplemented by thinking drawn not only from sociology, anthropology, and semiotics, but also from gender and postcolonial studies. In a turn towards what is sometimes called the hermeneutics of suspicion, attention settled on music's role in legitimizing power and social injustice, with traditional aesthetic approaches to music—approaches that see it as concerned solely with universal values of beauty—being seen (again in Bhabha's phrase) as masking ethnocentric norms, values, and interests.

Music is a powerful force in both personal and social life, and understanding its effects is as important a skill for navigating today's world as understanding the potential for deception inherent in photography or deepfake video. It is part of contemporary media literacy. One might argue that the slashing of school music provision in the UK that resulted from the austerity agenda and the rolling back of the state deprives young people of such skills, as well as helping to transform music into an enclave of privilege. And we need to remember that for every 'us' that music helps to foster there is also a 'them', as illustrated by Powell and the alt-right or by the flute and drum bands of unionist parades in Northern Ireland. Yet suspicion can go too far. Against these negative examples we might cite, for example, the role of 'Nkosi Sikelel' iAfrica' as a symbol and facilitator of the unity of purpose that helped put an end to apartheid in South Africa. We might think of the many people who say joining a choir has changed their life (and there are said to be more choirs in Britain today than fish-and-chip shops). We might think of the entire field of music therapy, in which trained practitioners employ music as a means of forging relationships with clients who suffer from a range of communicative or other disorders. Or we might simply consider the pleasure music gives. As I said, music is not inherently good or bad. Its powers can be harnessed for better or for worse.

But then, for every academic who is too suspicious of music, there is a journalist who is too uncritical. 'Music is a force for change, for good and, yes, for harmony', read a leading article from

The Guardian in 2006; it spoke of 'young people from communities which, though apparently hopelessly divided, have come together to make music and, in the process, understand more about each other and each other's cultures'. It was talking about the West–Eastern Divan Orchestra, co-founded by Edward Said and Daniel Barenboim in 1999 as a means of promoting mutual understanding between Palestinians and Israelis, and made up of Arab, Jewish, and Spanish students. The utopian principle underlying it is one of mutual dependence: in Barenboim's words, 'an orchestra requires musicians to listen to each other; none should attempt to play louder than the next, they must respect and know each other'. For a time the orchestra was the media's darling, its achievements much hyped, even as its critics pointed out that many of the students treated it as a passport out of the Middle East and that it diverted funding from less high-profile but more sustainable initiatives on the ground. Barenboim himself, however, was more modest in his assessment of what the orchestra could achieve. In 2004, after the orchestra's famous concert in Ramallah, he said that it 'did not end the conflict. Yet, at least for a couple of hours, it managed to reduce the level of hatred to zero.'

In the same way, we should recognize music's potential not by making excessive claims for it but through acknowledging its well-documented personal and social value. And it's the same with music's potential for cross-cultural communication in a global world that is nevertheless beset with suspicion and misunderstanding. We saw the Eurocentrism underlying Stockhausen's claim, in his article on *Weltmusik*, that 'a European can experience Balinese music, a Japanese music from Mozambique, and a Mexican music from India'. Without some effort at understanding it on its own terms, Europeans may experience Balinese music only on theirs, so appropriating it to their world view rather than accepting and engaging with its otherness—and so, according to the music philosopher Stephen Davies, someone who listens to Balinese music but does not anticipate what might come next, or experience a sense of closure at the end, is interested 'not in the music, but in the noise it makes'. The logic is impeccable but there is a danger of throwing out the baby with the bathwater. For one thing, on Davies's criteria, we might have to say a lot of listeners to Western music, too, are interested not in the music but the noise it makes—but do we really want to say that? And for another, even if music is not a universal language, it can afford pleasure and a sense of common humanity that crosses cultural boundaries in a way that real languages cannot. Listening to a recording of Balinese music can do that, and it can also stimulate the effort to learn about it on its own terms and so achieve the kind of informed cross-cultural understanding Davies has in mind.

But here I must acknowledge that Daly has a point. Humans are social animals, and music has its greatest potential for meaning when we experience it with other people. That might mean a massed performance of 'Nkosi Sikelel' iAfrica' in the dying days of the apartheid regime; it might mean that Swedish choir member hearing the voices around her and feeling herself merged with the music; it might just mean listening to music with a significant other. However fleetingly, musical intimacy brings people together. Ultimately it is not a matter of understanding in Davies's sense. It is a matter of musically shared humanity.

References

All recordings referred to can be found on Spotify or YouTube at the time of writing. I provide search terms for Spotify, and urls for YouTube videos, only where searching is not straightforward.

Introduction

Prudential commercial: <https://www.youtube.com/watch?v=Z_0Takot9eM> (all urls accessed 15 September 2020).

Chapter 1: Music in the moment

Small, *Musicking: The Meanings of Performing and Listening* (Middletown, CT: Wesleyan University Press, 1998). Sartre, *Psychology of the Imagination* (London: Methuen, 1972), 224.

Steinhardt, *Indivisible by Four: A String Quartet in Pursuit of Harmony* (New York: Farrar Straus Giroux, 1998). He refers to the Quartet in G major K 327, but there is no such quartet; the only mature one in G major is K 387.

Schutz, 'Making music together: A study in social relationship', in Arvid Brodersen (ed.), *Collected Papers II: Studies in Social Theory* (The Hague: Martinus Nijhoff, 1967), 159–78 [175].

Ingold and Hallam (eds), 'Creativity and cultural improvisation: An introduction', in Elizabeth Hallam and Tim Ingold (eds), *Creativity and Cultural Improvisation* (Oxford: Berg, 2007), 1–24 [6, 10–11, 19].

Gergen, *Relational Being: Beyond Self and Community* (New York: Oxford University Press, 2009), 30.

Brown quote: Arthur Knight, 'Jammin' the blues, or the sight of jazz, 1944', in Krin Gabbard (ed.), *Representing Jazz* (Durham, NC: Duke University Press, 1995), 11–53 [16]. Sidran, *Black Talk* (New York: Holt, Rinehart and Winston, 1971), 6.

Boulez quote: Michael Oliver, *Settling the Score: A Journey through the Music of the Twentieth Century* (London: Faber, 1999), 147.

Mingus quote: Barry Kernfeld, *What to Listen for in Jazz* (New Haven: Yale University Press, 1995), 119. Nettl quote: *The Study of Ethnomusicology: Twenty-nine Issues and Concepts* (Urbana: University of Illinois Press, 1983), 40.

Berliner, *Thinking in Jazz: The Infinite Art of Improvisation* (Chicago: University of Chicago Press, 1994), 102. Nooshin, 'Improvisation as "other": Creativity, knowledge and power—The case of Iranian classical music', *Journal of the Royal Musical Association* 128/2 (2003), 242–96 [277].

Armstrong's solos: Lawrence Gushee, 'The improvisation of Louis Armstrong', in Bruno Nettl with Melinda Russell (eds), *In the Course of Performance: Studies in the World of Musical Improvisation* (Chicago: University of Chicago Press, 1998), 291–334.

Schoenberg on performers: Dika Newlin, *Schoenberg Remembered: Diaries and Recollections (1938–76)* (New York: Pendragon Press, 1980), 164.

Philip, *Early Recordings and Musical Style: Changing Tastes in Instrumental Performance, 1900–1950* (Cambridge: Cambridge University Press, 1992), 220.

Core articles on early music: Leech-Wilkinson, 'What we are doing with early music is genuinely authentic to such a small degree that the word loses most of its intended meaning', *Early Music* 12/1 (1984), 13–16; Taruskin, 'The pastness of the present and the presence of the past', in *Text and Act: Essays on Music and Performance* (New York: Oxford University Press, 1995), 90–154 (originally published 1988).

Austin, *How to Do Things with Words: The William James Lectures delivered at Harvard University in 1955* (Oxford: Clarendon Press, 1962).

Hodge, 'Aesthetic decomposition: Music, identity, and time', in Michael Krausz (ed.), *The Interpretation of Music: Philosophical Essays* (Oxford: Clarendon Press, 1993), 247–58 (includes discussion of Wittgenstein).

Music

Solie, 'Whose life? The gendered self in Schumann's *Frauenliebe* songs', in Stephen Paul Scher (ed.), *Music and Text: Critical Inquiries* (Cambridge: Cambridge University Press, 1992), 219–40.

Potter, *Vocal Authority: Singing Style and Ideology* (Cambridge: Cambridge University Press, 1998), 182.

Swedish choir member: Alf Gabrielsson, *Strong Experiences with Music: Music is much more than just music* (Oxford: Oxford University Press, 2011), 251.

Meintjes, 'The politics of the recording studio: A case study from South Africa', in Nicholas Cook et al. (eds), *The Cambridge Companion to Recorded Music* (Cambridge: Cambridge University Press, 2009), 84–97 [85].

Management studies approach to music: Yaakov Atik, 'The conductor and the orchestra: Interactive aspects of the leadership process', *Leadership and Organization Development Journal* 15/1 (1994), 22–8.

Chapter 2: Thinking in music

Rumi quoted in Hasan Shah, *The Dancing Girl* (New York: New Directions, 1993), 93. Costello quote: Timothy White, 'A man out of time beats the clock', *Musician* 60 (October 1983), 52. Seeger, *Studies in Musicology 1935–75* (Berkeley: University of California Press, 1977), 45.

Kingsbury, *Music, Talent, and Performance: A Conservatory Cultural System* (Philadelphia: Temple University Press, 1988), 181.

Talk and wine: Adrienne Lehrer, *Wine and Conversation* (New York: Oxford University Press, 2009).

Ellena, *Perfume: The Alchemy of Scent* (New York: Arcade Publishing, 2011), 38.

Scruton, *The Aesthetics of Architecture* (London: Methuen, 1979), 51.

Borges, 'Of exactitude in science', in *A Universal History of Infamy* (London: Allen Lane, 1973), 141.

Figure 6: thanks to Susan Rankin for helping me over this, as well as allowing me to reproduce her transcription.

Kangxi emperor: Shubing Jia, *The Dissemination of Western Music through Catholic Missions in High Qing China (1662–1795)* (PhD dissertation, University of Bristol, 2012), 32.

Sudnow, *Talk's Body: A Meditation between Two Keyboards* (New York: Knopf, 1979), 6–7.

Clark, *Supersizing the Mind: Embodiment, Action, and Cognitive Extension* (New York: Oxford University Press, 2008), 2.

Notes in South Indian singing: Robert Gjerdingen, 'Shape and motion in the microstructure of song', *Music Perception* 6 (1988), 35–64.

Bamberger, 'Turning music theory on its ear: Do we hear what we see? Do we see what we say?', *International Journal of Computers for Mathematical Learning* 1 (1996), 33–55 [40].

Harrison quote from Eric Clarke et al., 'Interpretation and performance in Bryn Harrison's *être-temps*', *Musicae Scientiae* 19 (2005), 31–74 [43].

Musicians' exaggerated claims: Marie Agnew, 'A comparison of the auditory images of musicians, psychologists and children', *Psychological Monographs* 31/1 (1922), 268–78.

Gorton and Östersjö: Eric Clarke et al., 'Fluid practices, solid roles? The evolution of *Forlorn Hope*', in Clarke and Mark Doffman (eds), *Distributed Creativity: Collaboration and Improvisation in Contemporary Music* (New York: Oxford University Press, 2018), 116–35; Östersjö's six-minute passage of improvisation at <https://global.oup.com/us/companion.websites/9780199355914/resources/video/ch6/> (first example); finished piece on Spotify.

Lang's ridiculous rules: Anne McCutchan, *The Muse that Sings: Composers Speak about the Creative Process* (New York: Oxford University Press, 1999), 222. Reynolds, *Form and Method: Composing Music* (New York: Routledge, 2002), 41. Ferneyhough: Ross Feller, 'E-sketches: Brian Ferneyhough's use of computer-assisted compositional tools', in Patricia Hall and Friedemann Sallis (eds), *A Handbook to Twentieth-Century Musical Sketches* (Cambridge: Cambridge University Press, 2004), 176–88.

Performing edition of Beethoven's piano concerto movement on Spotify (search on 'Hess 15'); see also Nicholas Cook, 'Beethoven's unfinished piano concerto: A case of double vision?', *Journal of the American Musicological Society*, 42 (1989), 38–74. The performing edition was prepared in collaboration with Kelina Kwan.

Feynman and Wiener: James Gleick, *Genius: Richard Feynman and Modern Physics* (London: Abacus, 1994), 409.

Music

Beethoven's advice on composing: letter 1203 in Emily Anderson (ed.), *The Letters of Beethoven*, 3 vols (London: Macmillan, 1961). Sketching in the woods: August von Klöber's account in [Alexander Wheelock] *Thayer's Life of Beethoven* (Princeton: Princeton University Press, 1967), 703.

Eno, 'The studio as compositional tool', in Christoph Cox and Daniel Warner (eds), *Audio Culture: Readings in Modern Music* (New York: Continuum, 2004), 127–30.

Merleau-Ponty, *Signs* (Evanston, IL: Northwestern University Press, 1964), 45.

Chapter 3: The presence of the past

Allanbrook, *Rhythmic Gesture in Mozart:* Le Nozze de Figaro *and* Don Giovanni (Chicago: University of Chicago Press, 1983), 6.

Haydn's quartet: description by Giuseppe Carpani in Edward Klorman, *Mozart's Music of Friends: Social Interplay in the Chamber Works* (Cambridge: Cambridge University Press, 2016), 41.

Boellstorff, *Coming of Age in Second Life* (Princeton: Princeton University Press, 2008), 201.

Lessing (writing about symphonies accompanying spoken drama) quoted in Wye Jamison Allanbrook, *The Secular Commedia: Comic Mimesis in Late Eighteenth-Century Music*, ed. Mary Ann Smart and Richard Taruskin (Berkeley: University of California Press, 2014), 24.

Critical notices of Beethoven's Ninth Symphony: details in Nicholas Cook, *Beethoven: Symphony No. 9* (Cambridge: Cambridge University Press, 1993), 23, 27 (Kanne), 70–1 (Fröhlich), 37–8.

New practices of listening: James Johnson, *Listening in Paris: A Cultural History* (Berkeley: University of California Press, 1996).

Wagner and Rolland: Cook, *Beethoven: Symphony No. 9*, 73 ('Joy through suffering' at 96).

Gjerdingen, *Music in the Galant Style* (New York: Oxford University Press, 2007), 7. Mark Evan Bonds investigates this phenomenon in *The Beethoven Syndrome: Hearing Music as Autobiography* (New York: Oxford University Press, 2020).

Solomon, *Beethoven* (London: Macmillan, 1997), 222–3.

'Judas' and the fan quote: Christopher Paul Lee, *Like the Night (revisited): Bob Dylan and the Road to the Manchester Free Trade*

Hall (London. Helter Skelter Publishing, 2004), 161. There is conflicting evidence about the heckler's identity and motivation.

Piganini/Cooder clip ('Music is more than technique') at <https://www.youtube.com/watch?v=JvLkt_0dPP8>.

Clara Schumann quote: Nancy Reich, *Clara Schumann: The Artist and Woman* (Ithaca, NY: Cornell University Press, 1985), 229.

Exposure of Schlösser and Rochlitz: Solomon, 'On Beethoven's creative process: A two-part invention', *Music & Letters* 61 (1980), 272–83 [275, 274]. Reger: Giselher Schubert and Friedmann Sallis, 'Sketches and sketching', in Hall and Sallis, *A Handbook to Twentieth-Century Musical Sketches*, 5–16 [7].

Bilson, 'Execution and expression in the Sonata in E flat, K 382', *Early Music* 20 (1992), 237–43.

Pitts, 'Reflection', in Daniel Leech-Wilkinson and Helen Prior (eds), *Music and Shape* (New York: Oxford University Press, 2017), 386–7 [386].

Abbate, 'Music—drastic or gnostic?', *Critical Inquiry* 30 (2004), 505–36 [512]; Leech-Wilkinson, 'Cortot's Berceuse', *Music Analysis* 34 (2015), 335–63 [345]. Leech-Wilkinson on the classical performance establishment: 'Classical music as enforced utopia', *Arts and Humanities in Higher Education* 15 (2016), 325–36.

Kramer on pale-faced audiences, *Classical Music and Postmodern Knowledge* (Berkeley: University of California Press, 1995), 3–4. Alex Ross, 'Why so serious?', *New Yorker*, 8 September 2008. Kramer on summer nights, *Why Classical Music Still Matters* (Berkeley: University of California Press, 2007), 2.

Birtwistle: Simon Barrow, NewFrontEars blog, 6 September 2003 (<http://newfrontears.blogspot.com/2003/09/180.html>).

Dylan box set: Ben Sisario, 'Dylan's 1996 tapes find a direction home', *New York Times*, 11 November 2016 (<https://www.nytimes.com/2016/11/11/arts/music/bob-dylan-1966-live-recordings-video.html>).

Beyoncé and lip-synching: '"Any Questions?" Beyonce admits to lip-syncing but silences her critics by doing this…', *Her* (<https://www.her.ie/celeb/any-questions-beyonce-admits-to-lip-syncing-but-silences-her-critics-by-doing-this-26779>). L'Oréal whitening her skin: Mark Sweney, 'Beyoncé Knowles: L'Oreal accused of "whitening" singer in cosmetics ad', *The Guardian*, 8 August 2008 (<https://www.theguardian.com/media/2008/aug/08/advertising.usa>).

Grande darkening her skin: Sabrina Barr, 'Ariana Grande accused of cultural appropriation by speaking with a "blaccent"', *The Independent*, 10 December 2018 (<https://www.independent.co.uk/life-style/ariana-grande-blaccent-thank-u-next-video-accent-cultural-appropriation-billboard-interview-a8675596.html>). Hall of Fame exhibit: Ryan Reed, 'Beyonce fashion exhibit coming to Rock and Roll Hall of Fame', *Rolling Stone*, 18 July 2014 (<https://www.rollingstone.com/culture/culture-news/beyonce-fashion-exhibit-coming-to-rock-and-roll-hall-of-fame-236180>).

Celebrity: Jo Littler, 'Adrift or ashore? *Desert Island Discs* and celebrity culture', in Julie Brown et al. (eds), *Defining the Discographic Self*: Desert Island Discs *in Context* (London: British Academy, 2017), 93–106 [94].

Billboard on *Lemonade*: Miriam Bale, 'Beyonce's "Lemonade" is a revolutionary work of black feminism: Critic's notebook', *Billboard* 25 April 2016 (<https://www.billboard.com/articles/news/7341839/beyonce-lemonade-black-feminism>). Beyoncé explained her aim for *Lemonade* in her 2017 Grammy Award acceptance speech. Beyoncé's costumes: Amy MacKeldan, 'Beyoncé's Coachella performance featured Destiny's Child, Jay Z, Solange, and several epic costume changes', *Harper's Bazaar*, 15 April 2018 (<https://www.harpersbazaar.com/culture/art-books-music/a19697446/beyonce-coachella-2018-performance/>).

Records reproducing works: Nick Morgan, '"A new pleasure": Listening to National Gramophonic Society records, 1924–1931', *Musicae Scientiae* 14 (2010), 139–64 [151].

Culshaw's innovative production: David Patmore and Eric Clarke, 'Making and hearing virtual worlds: John Culshaw and the art of record production', *Musicae Scientiae* 11 (2007), 269–93 (to hear his recordings on Spotify search for 'Solti Ring'). Gould's innovative production (e.g. of Jean Sibelius's *Kyllikki*): Kevin Bazzana, *Glenn Gould: The Performer in the Work* (Oxford: Oxford University Press, 1997).

G-funk and in-car listening: Justin Williams, '"Cars with the boom": Music, automobility, and hiphop "sub" cultures', in Sumanth Gopinath and Jason Stanyek (eds), *The Oxford Handbook of Mobile Music Studies* (New York: Oxford University Press, 2014), vol. 2, 109–45 [126].

References

Rousseau, *Essay on the Origin of Languages* (1781), available in multiple translations.

Savage, *Bytes and Backbeats: Repurposing Music in the Digital Age* (Ann Arbor: University of Michigan Press, 2011), 53.

Krims, *Music and Urban Geography* (New York: Routledge, 2007), 144, 136, 146, 149; Bach recording is Organ Concerto Wq. 34 with Christine Schornsheim and the Akademie für Alte Musik (search 'Bach Schornsheim Wq. 34'), Anonymous 4 ones are *American Angels* and *The Origin of Fire*.

Björk's *Biophilia* app, Hough's Liszt app, and Augment app available from the Apple App Store; Augment web page <http://augment.audio/>.

Christgau blog ('Xgau sez'): <http://www.robertchristgau.com/xgausez.php?d=2018-11-20>.

Affective recommendation based on selfies: Sumanth Gopinath and Jason Stanyek, 'Techniques of the musical selfie', in Nicholas Cook et al. (eds), *The Cambridge Companion to Music in Digital Culture* (Cambridge: Cambridge University Press, 2019), 89–118 [96].

Spotify's 'Daily Wellness': <https://newsroom.spotify.com/2020-04-27/daily-wellness-a-new-mix-of-motivational-podcasts-and-personalized-music/>.

Koester blog, 16 September 2016: <http://www.markwk.com/2016/09/tracking-music-listening.html>.

Geertz, *Local Knowledge: Essays in Interpretive Anthropology* (New York: Basic Books, 1983), 59.

Figure for Miku's YouTube videos from <https://ec.crypton.co.jp/pages/prod/vocaloid/cv01_us>; fan's comments from Rafal Zaborowski, 'Hatsune Miku and Japanese virtual idols', in Sheila Whiteley and Shara Rambarran (eds), *The Oxford Handbook of Music and Virtuality* (New York: Oxford University Press, 2016), 111–28 [123].

Whitacre's 'Fly to Paradise' remix site: <https://ericwhitacre.com/the-virtual-choir/history/vc4-flytoparadise-remix>.

Finnegan, *The Hidden Musicians: Music-Making in an English Town*, 2nd edn (Middletown, CT: Wesleyan University Press, 2007).

Cook, 'Video cultures: "Bohemian Rhapsody", *Wayne's World*, and beyond', in Joshua Walden (ed.), *Representation in Western Music* (Cambridge: Cambridge University Press, 2013), 79–99.

Music

WELL: Howard Rheingold, *The Virtual Community: Homesteading on the Electronic Frontier* (Reading, MA: Addison-Wesley, 1993).

Jenkins, *Convergence Culture: Where Old and New Media Collide* (New York: New York University Press, 2006); Jenkins's grandmother: Jenkins et al., *Participatory Culture in a Networked Era* (Cambridge: Polity Press, 2016), 7–8.

Turino, *Music as Social Life: The Politics of Participation* (Chicago: University of Chicago Press, 2008).

Shifman, *Memes in Digital Culture* (Cambridge, MA: MIT Press, 2014).

Original video of *Nyan Cat* at https://www.youtube.com/watch?v=QH2-TGUlwu4&list=PLbRUzU8R_JMJ68MGQ9PJHYS4TxD29jwVu. Information on *Nyan Cat* at <https://knowyourmeme.com/memes/nyan-cat>.

Richardson, *An Eye for Music: Popular Music and the Audiovisual Surreal* (New York: Oxford University Press, 2012), 171.

Jenkins et al., *Spreadable Media: Creating Value and Meaning in a Networked Culture* (New York: New York University, 2013).

Rolland, *Beethoven* (London: Kegan Paul, 1919), 47.

Figures for Napster users from Michael Gowan, 'Requiem for Napster', *PC World*, 18 May 2002 (<https://www.pcworld.idg.com.au/article/22380/requiem_napster/>); for music industry litigation from Mark Katz, *Capturing Sound: How Technology has Changed Music* (Berkeley: University of California Press, 2004), 176 and 'Minnesota woman ordered to pay $222,000 in music piracy case', *Rolling Stone*, 12 September 2012 (<https://www.rollingstone.com/music/music-news/minnesota-woman-ordered-to-pay-222000-in-music-piracy-case-236366/>). Lessig, *Remix: Making Art and Commerce Thrive in the Hybrid Economy* (London: Bloomsbury, 2008), 114; Jenkins quote from *Convergence Culture*, 163–4.

Increased legal purchases: Katz, *Capturing Sound*, 169. iTunes accounts: Rhiannon Williams, 'What does iTunes closing down mean for my music collection?', *iNews*, 4 June 2019 (<https://inews.co.uk/news/technology/wwdc-2019-itunes-has-been-officially-replaced-by-apple-music-tv-and-podcasts-500983>).

Bandcamp customers paying over the odds: Selling FAQ 'What pricing performs best?' (<https://get.bandcamp.help/hc/en-us/articles/360007802534-What-pricing-performs-best->).

Bush's iPod playlist: e.g. Elisabeth Bullimer, 'White House letter: President Bush's iPod', *New York Times*, 11 April 2005 (<https://

www.nytimes.com/2005/04/11/politics/white-house-letterpresident-
bushs-ipod.html>).

Spotify's playlists for sex: Alex Hern, 'Spotify knows what music you're
having sex to', *The Guardian*, 13 February 2015 (<https://www.
theguardian.com/technology/2015/feb/13/spotify-knows-what-
music-youre-having-sex-to>).

Spotify's Privacy Policy (25 May 2018), <https://www.spotify.com/uk/
legal/privacy-policy-update/?_ga=2.210533909.141856396.
1599498539-203562537.1524838649>. Google knowing you are
pregnant: Bill Thompson, 'The net reveals the ties that bind',
BBC News, 17 November 2008 (<http://news.bbc.co.uk/2/hi/
technology/7733368.stm>). Spotify's pledge (from its 2015 media
kit): Eric Drott, 'Music as a technology of surveillance', *Journal of
the Society for American Music* 12/3 (2018), 233–67 [258].
Rheingold quote, *The Virtual Community*, 297.

Chapter 5: Music in a global world

Father Gnecchi: Eta Harich-Schneider, *A History of Japanese Music*
(London: Oxford University Press, 1973), 457. Eighteenth-century
Calcutta: Raymond Head, 'Corelli in Calcutta: Colonial music-making
in India during the 17th and 18th centuries', *Early Music* 13/4
(1985), 548–53; Ian Woodfield, *Music of the Raj: A Social and
Economic History of Music in Late Eighteenth-Century Anglo-Indian
Society* (Oxford: Oxford University Press, 2000).

Mozart and Haydn: Karl Geiringer, *Joseph Haydn: A Creative Life in
Music*, 3rd edn (Berkeley: University of California Press, 1982), 98.

Rio newspaper article: *L'Écho*, 3 October 1827, quoted in Ben
Walton, 'Listening through the operatic voice in 1820s Rio de
Janeiro', in Peter McMurray and Priyasha Mukhopadhyay (eds),
Acoustics of Empire (New York: Oxford University Press,
forthcoming); thanks to Ben Walton for permission to use his
translation. Bowdich quote (discussed by James Davies in a
chapter from the same book) from Thomas Bowditch, *Mission
from Cape Coast Castle to Ashantee* (London: John Murray 1819),
451. Bhabha quote from Jonathan Rutherford, 'The third space:
Interview with Homi Bhabha', in Jonathan Rutherford (ed.),
Identity: Community, Culture, Difference (London: Lawrence &
Wishart, 1998), 207–21 [208].

Powell: Rolf Charlston, 'A rhapsodic *Heart of Darkness*: John Powell's
Rhapsodie Nègre', *The Conradian* 26/2 (2001), 79–90 and Lester

Feder, 'Unequal temperament: The somatic acoustics of racial difference in the symphonic music of John Powell', *Black Music Research Journal* 28/1 (2008), 17–56.

Tike Taane: Wilson, 'Tiki Taane's *With Strings Attached: Alive and Orchestrated* and postcolonial identity politics in New Zealand', in Tina Ramnarine (ed.), *Global Orchestras* (New York: Oxford University Press, 2018), 245–60 [248].

Erhu performance: I am drawing on Jonathan Stock, *Musical Creativity in Twentieth-Century China: Abing, his Music, and its Changing Meanings* (Rochester, NY: Rochester University Press, 1996).

Takemitsu, 'Contemporary music in Japan', *Perspectives of New Music* 27/2 (1989), 198–204 [199].

For White power and alt-right music see Wikipedia ('White power music', 'National Socialist black metal').

Listing of metal bands by country: Metal Archives (<https://www.metal-archives.com/browse/country>), and distribution map (<https://www.altpress.com/news/the_distribution_of_heavy_metal_bands_around_the_world_according_to_guardia/>); downloads, Kevin Cornell, 'Tunecore artists hit cash record: $1.5 billion in revenue', TuneCore News, 29 April 2019 (<https://www.tunecore.com/blog/2019/04/tunecore-artists-hit-cash-record-1-5-billion-in-revenue.html>).

Papers from the Empress of Russia meetings: <https://frootsmag.com/world-music-history-minutes-and-press-releases>. Agawu, *Representing African Music: Postcolonial Notes, Queries, Positions* (New York: Routledge, 2003), 6.

Weltmusik: Björn Heile, '*Weltmusik* and the globalization of new music', in Heile (ed.), *The Modernist Legacy: Essays on New Music* (Farnham: Ashgate, 2009), 101–21; Stockhausen, *Texte zur Musik 1970–1977* (Cologne: DuMont, 1978), 468–76 (translation by Tim Nevill and Suzanne Stephens, formerly at <http://www.stockhausen.org/stockhausen_texts.html>). Schoenberg on the supremacy of German music: Hans Heinz Stuckenschmidt, *Arnold Schoenberg: His Life, World and Work* (London: Calder, 1977), 277.

Chou, 'East and West, old and new', *Asian Music* 1/1 (1968–9), 19–22, and 'Asian esthetics and world music', in Harrison Rykert (ed.), *New Music in the Orient* (Buren: Frits Knupf, 1991), 177–87 [177].

Scott quote: 'Cosmopolitan musicology', in Elaine Kelley et al. (eds), *Confronting the National in the Musical Past* (London: Routledge, 2018), 17–30 [18–19].

Daly quoted in Laurent Aubert, *The Music of the Other: New Challenges for Ethnomusicology in a Global Age* (Aldershot. Ashgate, 2007), 55.

Tolkien, *The Lord of the Rings* (London: HarperCollins, 1994), 564.

Horkheimer, *Critical Theory: Selected Essays* (New York: Continuum, 1982), 244.

Singing changing people's lives, fish and chip shops: Caroline Bithell, *A Different Voice, a Different Song* (New York: Oxford University Press, 2014), 14, 20.

Leading article, 'Barenboim's harmonious message goes beyond classical music', *The Guardian*, 30 April 2006, at <https://www.theguardian.com/commentisfree/2006/apr/30/arts.classicalmusicandopera>; quotes from Barenboim at <https://danielbarenboim.com/daniel-barenboim-and-edward-said-upon-receiving-the-principe-de-asturias-prize/> and <https://danielbarenboim.com/speech-given-by-daniel-barenboim-upon-receiving-the-buber-rosenzweig-medal-at-the-week-of-fraternity-2004/>; critique by Rachel Beckles Willson, 'The parallax worlds of the West-Eastern Divan Orchestra', *Journal of the Royal Musical Association* 134/2 (2009), 319–47.

Davies, *Musical Meaning and Expression* (Ithaca, NY: Cornell University Press, 1994), 326.

Further reading

Much of this book draws on my own research, presented more fully in the following publications: *Music as Creative Practice* (New York: Oxford University Press, 2018), relevant to Chapters 1–3; *Beyond the Score: Music as Performance* (New York: Oxford University Press, 2013), relevant to Chapter 1 (also on recording, Chapters 3–4); 'Digital technology and cultural practice', in Nicholas Cook et al. (eds), *The Cambridge Companion to Music in Digital Culture* (Cambridge: Cambridge University Press, 2019), 5–28, relevant to Chapter 4 (for which the whole volume is a useful source); 'Western music as world music', in Philip Bohlman (ed.), *The Cambridge History of World Music* (Cambridge: Cambridge University Press, 2013), 75–99, relevant to Chapter 5 (again the whole volume is a useful source).

At the time of writing, other volumes of the *Very Short Introduction* series cover Early music, Film music, The Blues, Country music, Folk music, World music, The Orchestra, Ethnomusicology, and Psychology of music. There aren't volumes on jazz or rock, but introductions to these include Ted Goia, *The History of Jazz*, 2nd edn (New York: Oxford University Press, 2013), and John Covach and Andrew Florey, *What's That Sound? An Introduction to Rock and its History*, 5th edn (New York: Norton, 2018).

Approachable introductions to Western music are Howard Goodall's *The Story of Music* (London: Chatto and Windus, 2013) and—specifically on the classical tradition—Julian Johnson's *Classical Music: A Beginner's Guide* (Oxford: Oneworld, 2009). One-volume histories of classical music include Mark Evan Bonds's *History of*

Music in Western Culture, 4th edn (Boston: Pearson, 2014) and, for the 20th century, Alex Ross's *The Rest is Noise: Listening to the Twentieth Century* (London: Fourth Estate, 2007). More extensive are Richard Taruskin's 3,856-page *Oxford History of Music* (New York: Oxford University Press, 2009, <https://www.oxfordwesternmusic.com/>) and the multi-authored volumes of the *Cambridge History of Music*, including both chronologically based volumes and topical ones on American music, Western music theory, World music, Musical performance, and Music criticism. Jonathan Sterne's *The Audible Past: Cultural Origins of Sound Reproduction* (Durham, NC: Duke University Press, 2003) shows how music technology relates to cultural history and the rapidly developing field of sound studies, on which Sterne has also edited an introductory collection: *The Sound Studies Reader* (Abingdon: Routledge, 2012).

Issues of classical music's role in contemporary society have been discussed from a musicological perspective in Julian Johnson's *Who Needs Classical Music?* (Cambridge: Cambridge University Press, 2003) and Lawrence Kramer's *Why Classical Music Still Matters* (Berkeley: University of California Press, 2007), and from a sociological one in David Hesmondhalgh's *Why Music Matters* (Malden, MA: Wiley-Blackwell, 2013).

J. P. E. Harper-Scott's and Jim Samson's co-edited book *An Introduction to Music Studies* (Cambridge: Cambridge University Press, 2009) is an introductory overview of topics and approaches in the academic study of music (my chapter, on the music business, enlarges on what I say in this book). Other sources introducing recent thinking in music studies include David Beard and Kenneth Gloag, *Musicology: The Key Concepts*, 2nd edn (Abingdon: Routledge, 2016) and two multi-author collections: Nicholas Cook and Mark Everist (eds), *Rethinking Music* (Oxford: Oxford University Press, 1999) and Martin Clayton et al. (eds), *The Cultural Study of Music: A Critical Introduction*, 2nd edn (New York: Routledge, 2012).

The literature on specific genres and topics in both Western and non-Western music is endless, but can be approached through various series of multi-authored volumes. One is the long-running *Cambridge Companions*, of which over 70 are about music; another is the *Oxford Handbooks* series, designed as an online library but also available in printed form.

A one-volume reference source, oriented towards classical music, is Alison Latham's *The Oxford Companion to Music* (Oxford: Oxford University Press, 2002). This is now part of Oxford Music Online (<https://www.oxfordmusiconline.com/>), along with *Grove Music Online*, the most authoritative and comprehensive English-language reference source for music (historically oriented towards the classical tradition but now becoming increasingly comprehensive). For world music a key online resource is the *Garland Encyclopedia of World Music*, originally published in ten volumes but now accessible at <http://glnd.alexanderstreet.com>.

Index

For the benefit of digital users, indexed terms that span two pages (e.g., 52–53) may, on occasion, appear on only one of those pages.

Music

EARLY MUSIC
A Very Short Introduction
Thomas Forrest Kelly

The music of the medieval, Renaissance, and baroque periods
have been repeatedly discarded and rediscovered ever since
they were new. In recent years interest in music of the past
has taken on particular meaning, representing two specific
trends: first, a rediscovery of little-known underappreciated
repertories, and second, an effort to recover lost performing
styles. In this VSI, Thomas Forrest Kelly frames chapters on
the forms, techniques, and repertories of the medieval,
Renaissance, and baroque periods with discussion of why old
music has been and should be revived, along with a short
history of early music revivals.

www.oup.com/vsi

FILM MUSIC
A Very Short Introduction
Kathryn Kalinak

This *Very Short Introduction* provides a lucid, accessible, and engaging overview of the subject of film music. Beginning with an analysis of the music from a well-known sequence in the film Reservoir Dogs, the book focuses on the most central issues in the practice of film music. Expert author Kay Kalinak takes readers behind the scenes to understand both the practical aspects of film music - what it is and how it is composed - and also the theories that have been developed to explain why film musicworks. This compact book not entertains with the fascinating stories of the composers and performers who have shaped film music across the globe but also gives readers a broad sense for the key questions in film music studies today.

'Kathryn Kalinak has emerged as one of the freshest and most authoritative commentary on film music of her generation.'

Michael Quinn, Classical Music